The Connecticut River

NEW ENGLAND'S HISTORIC WATERWAY

BY EDMUND DELANEY

The Globe Pequot Press

CHESTER, CONNECTICUT 06412

The publisher gratefully acknowledges the Connecticut River Foundation for the use of the painting, *Steamboat Dock, Essex, 1881* by Richard L. Brooks, on the cover.

Library of Congress Cataloging in Publication Data
Delaney, Edmund T. (Edmund Thomas), 1914-
    The Connecticut River, New England's historic waterway.

    Includes index.
    1. Connecticut River — History. 2. Connecticut River Valley—History. I. Title
F12.C7D44 1983   974.6   83-80635
ISBN 0-87106-980-6 (pbk.)

Manufactured in the United States of America
First Edition

Text design by Herman Dean

PREFACE

I have long been fascinated with the Connecticut River, which I first came to know some fifty years ago when I spent summers in Vermont. In the ensuing years, I have crossed and recrossed it countless times. I have sailed its tidewaters for many summers and have had personal encounters with its many sandbars. And yet, it was only when I came to Chester on its southern banks that I came fully to appreciate not only its extraordinary beauty, but also its rich historical associations. This book represents an endeavor to share all of this bounty with others, many of whom will have an equal attachment to the *Quinnetukut,* as it was called by the Indians before the white men arrived.

For valuable suggestions, good criticisms, and sound advice, I am indebted to Belton A. Copp, Ellsworth S. Grant, and Burton Powers. Others who have read the manuscript and have made constructive comments include Curtiss S. Johnson, Kelso F. Davis, and the late Thomas A. Stevens of the Connecticut River Foundation at Steamboat Dock in Essex; John Crosman, Christopher Percy, and Terry Blunt of the Connecticut River Watershed Council of Easthampton, Mass. Russell L. Brenneman, and the late Robert Wilkerson.

All the curators and archivists from whom I have received pictures were most helpful. Special thanks are due to Melancthon W. Jacobus of the Connecticut Historical Society (not only for the pictures, but also for much background information contained in his splendid book, *The Connecticut River Steamboat Story),* Brenda Milkofsky of the Connecticut River Foundation, Dominick J. Ruggiero of the Connecticut Department of Economic Development, Dr. Albert E. Van Dusen, Connecticut State Historian, Kenneth Cramer and Barbara Krieger of Dartmouth College Library, Nancy E. Boone of the Vermont Division of Historic Preservation, Blaise Bisaillon and Angela Sciotti of the Forbes Memorial Library in Northampton, William Hosley of the Wadsworth Atheneum, William Copeley of the New Hampshire Historical Society, Pamela Hodgkins of Historic Deerfield, Jeffrey Anderson and Barbara MacAdam of the Lyme Historical Society, Robert Clark of the Wesleyan Public Relations Department, Sylvie Carrier of the Greater Springfield Chamber of Commerce, and Russell D'Oench of the Middletown Press.

My appreciation is also expressed to Ellen Paterson and Marion Carpenter, who typed and retyped the manuscript.

Most of all, however, I want to pay tribute to the painstaking labors of Cary Hull, my gifted editor, for her work in the organization of the book and her constructive criticisms and suggestions with respect to its contents.

Chester, Connecticut,   Edmund Delaney
June 1, 1983

Dedicated to my wife,
Barbara,
with thanks for her help, interest, and patience

CONTENTS

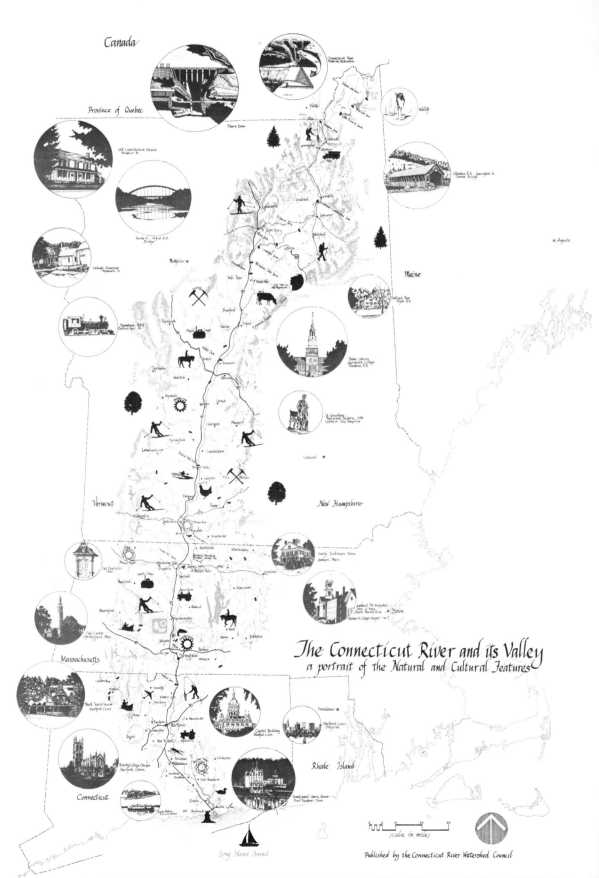

The Connecticut River and its Valley
a portrait of the Natural and Cultural Features

scale in miles

Published by the Connecticut River Watershed Council

CREDITS: PUBLISHED WITH A GRANT FROM THE HOWARD AND BUSH FOUNDATION, HARTFORD, CT. • DONATIONS BY GENERAL OFFSET PRINTING, INC., SPRINGFIELD, MA. • TAN LINWEAVE® TEXT BY BROWN CO., LINWEAVE DIV., HOLYOKE, MA. • STONINGTON TUBE CORP., EASTHAMPTON, MA. • GRAPHICS BY NACUL CENTER, AMHERST, MA. • PROJECT ORGANIZATION BY CURRAN ASSOC., NORTHAMPTON, MA. • COPYRIGHT 1976, CONNECTICUT RIVER WATERSHED COUNCIL, INC. 125 COMBS. RD., EASTHAMPTON, MA. 01027 • A NON-PROFIT MEMBERSHIP CONSERVATION ORGANIZATION • $5.00

1

THE RIVER

Connecticut, the most considerable river in the eastern part of the United States, has its source in a pond in the highlands which separate the states of Vermont and New Hampshire from Lower Canada.

The American Gazetteer of 1810
Jedidiah Morse

Americans like to judge things by size, with the ultimate accolade going to the biggest, the tallest, the widest, or the deepest. By any such superlatives, the Connecticut River does not measure up. In no way as long as the Missouri, nor as wide as the Mississippi, nor as majestic as the Hudson, nor as colorful as the Colorado winding its way through the Grand Canyon, the Connecticut must be content to be judged only by New England standards, under which it is indeed the longest — 410 miles — and, at its mouth, the widest.

And yet, measured by the subjective standards of beauty of those who love it, the Connecticut River yields to none. In the early nineteenth century, Yale President Timothy Dwight, who was born in Northampton on the Massachusetts reach of the river, wrote in his *Travels in New-England and New-York:*

> This stream may, with more propriety than any other in the world, be named THE BEAUTIFUL RIVER. From Stuart, a few miles from its source, to the Sound it uniformly maintains this character. The purity, salubrity and sweetness of its waters; the frequency and elegance of its meanders; its absolute freedom from aquatic vegetables; the uncommon and universal beauty of its banks, here a smooth and winding beach, there covered with rich verdure, now fringed with bushes, now covered with lofty trees, and now formed by the intruding hill, the rude bluff and the shaggy mountain, are objects which no traveler can thoroughly describe and no reader can adequately imagine.

The name Connecticut is derived from the Indian designation of *Quonehtacut,* or *Quinatucquet,* or *Quenticut* (the English did not concern themselves too much with the spelling of Indian names), meaning "long tidal river" or "long estuary." Obviously, it was from the river that the state received its name.

For a small river, the Connecticut is particularly rich in history. In its early days, it was the main avenue of transportation for all of New England. It was also the route to the sea, and the towns on its shores had uninterrupted access to the channels of commerce all along the shores of Long Island Sound. With its rich natural resources and fertile flood plain, the river valley became the center of New England agriculture. The water power of the river and its tributaries was responsible for the Industrial

Revolution and growth of many of the towns along its banks, and for a large part of New England's energy resources. It was on the Connecticut that the steamboat was invented and the first submarine was launched. All along its shores are innumerable reminders of its long and exciting history and of the great personalities who, for over a period of 350 years, have had a profound impact upon American life.

The sources of the river are in New Hampshire, but a few hundred yards from the Canadian border. Little streams emanate from the mountain peaks, cross swamps and bogs, and then flow into three lakes, each named Connecticut, but distinguished by numbers. The third and northernmost lake, considered to be the real source of the river, is one mile long; the second is slightly larger with two point seventy-five miles, and the first lake covers four miles. Each lake has been artificially extended by dams built in the 1930s. From the first lake, the river flows into Lake Francis, a manmade lake created in 1940 when New Hampshire built a one hundred-foot dam at its western end.

The river is the boundary between New Hampshire and Vermont. The northernmost town on the river is Pittsburg, New Hampshire, which covers almost 300 square miles. It is situated on the western end of Lake Francis, near the convergence of Indian Stream and the Connecticut. Only in recent years opened up to the automobile traveler, this is a region of wilderness, a land for the fisherman, the hunter, the canoeist, and the nature lover. In the winter, covered as it is with snow, it has become a vast track for the snowmobile. This is also the area which declared itself the Independent Republic of Indian Stream in 1832, complete with its own president and constitution, but it was taken over by New Hampshire ten years later.

The river, marked by many rapids and gorges, and augmented by feeder streams, reaches the Vermont border at Beecher Falls. Passing Colebrook and Stratford on the New Hampshire side and Lemington and Bloomfield on the Vermont side, it enters the Coos country, an old Indian name meaning "the place of the curved river," although, in fact, the Connecticut curves throughout its entire course.

The Coos region is a rich valley covering some one hundred miles, with fertile meadows and gentle rolling hills edged by the White Mountains on the east and the Green Mountains to the west. Not without reason, this region is sometimes called the "Garden of New England."

At Northumberland, the river twists, turns, and meanders through the valley, forming a beautiful oxbow. From Lancaster, a bucolic town in rich farmland, there is a magnificent view of the surrounding Presidential Range of the White Mountains, including Mount Washington, 6,288 feet high.

Picking up more feeder streams on each side, the river is enlarged and enriched, spilling over a series of dams, some of which produce most of the electrical energy in New England: Guildhall-Northumberland, Gilman, Moore, Comerford, McIndoes Falls, and Ryegate.

Caledonia County on the Vermont side of the river is one of the three northeastern Vermont counties sometimes called the Northeast Kingdom. One town, Barnet, was originally settled by immigrants from Scotland, who gave the county its name. It was once hoped that steamboats could travel all the way upriver to Barnet, and there was a much-heralded at-

The uppermost Connecticut Lake on the border of New Hampshire and the Province of Quebec is the source of the river. In 1959, Dr. Joseph Davidson, President of the Connecticut River Watershed Council, and his wife dramatized on film the polluted condition of the river by traveling from its source to its mouth. Their film was for use in a public campaign to clean up the river.

The second Connecticut Lake covers 2.75 miles.

The dam at the western end of Lake Francis was originally
constructed as a flood control and storage reservoir facility, with
a potential for the creation of hydroelectric power.

The reservoir created by the Wilder Dam at Hanover, New Hampshire has
provided an excellent boating area for canoeists, sailors, and
Dartmouth College oarsmen. The college can be seen in the center background.

tempt in 1826 by a steamboat optimistically named the *Barnet,* but there were too many river obstructions. Barnet has been content to rest with the produce of its rich dairy farms.

Taking in the Wells River and Ammonoosuc River at Woodsville, the river flows through the valley of rural Vermont and New Hampshire. This is a valley of pastoral hillsides with cows, sheep, and red barns, and quiet villages with country stores, white steepled churches and meeting houses, white frame houses, and village greens with Civil War monuments and bandstands. It is an area renowned for its seasonal contrasts: the green foliage covering the hills in the summer; the autumnal reds, oranges, and yellows; the winter snow portrayed on so many Christmas cards; and the ever-renewing spring with its blossoms and wild flowers covering the countryside.

From Wells River to White River Junction, some forty miles south, is the so-called Lower Coos Country. This is a rich countryside with well-tended farms and fertile fields. The towns along the riverbanks are particularly attractive: Newbury, Bradford, Fairlee, the Thetfords, and Norwich in Vermont, and Haverhill, Orford, Lyme, and Hanover in New Hampshire. At Newbury, the river makes a four-mile loop at the "Great Oxbow" before it returns to a spot less than one-half mile from its original course. North of White River Junction is the Wilder Dam, which creates a reservoir extending thirty-five miles back to Newbury. Norwich and Hanover mark the river crossing for the Appalachian Trail.

As the river flows southward, picking up more volume from its tributaries, there are large towns every fifteen or twenty miles along the river: Windsor, Claremont, Springfield, Bellows Falls, and Brattleboro, all small enclaves of light industry. Along the way the river joins with the White River and the Ottauqueches River with its splendid Quechee Gorge. It flows past Windsor, in the shadow of Mount Ascutney, the highest peak in the Connecticut River Valley at 3,144 feet. The river almost touches Springfield, where it meets with the Black River flowing down from the Green Mountains. Pouring over the dam at Bellows Falls, it passes the Indian Petroglyphs, Indian carvings by members of the Pennacook tribe, made on the rocks along the riverbanks below the falls. The river continues past several picturesque towns in rolling hills and rich dairy country: Putney and Westminster in Vermont, and Chesterfield, Westmoreland, and Walpole in New Hampshire. Of Putney, Senator George D. Aiken, who lived there for many years, said: "I call it the intellectual center of the world. It's where people from Harvard come to get the rust rubbed off."

The river joins with the West River at Brattleboro and then with the Ashuelot at Hinsdale, New Hampshire. Across from Hinsdale is Vernon, the first town in a flat, rich alluvial flood plain that extends through Massachusetts and all the way down to Middletown, Connecticut. In Vernon, there are large farms as well as the Vermont Yankee Nuclear Plant.

The Connecticut River enters Massachusetts, bisecting it from north to south, with two-thirds of the state on its eastern side. The upper reaches of the river in Massachusetts are studded with an extraordinary conglomeration of educational institutions: Mount Holyoke College at South Hadley; Smith College and the Clark School for the Deaf (where Alexander Graham Bell was a teacher and board president) in Northampton;

Mount Sugarloaf, south of Greenfield, Massachusetts, overlooks
the flat, fertile flood plains of Pioneer Valley.

Amherst College, The University of Massachusetts, and Hampshire College in Amherst; and two community colleges in Holyoke and Greenfield. On the secondary level there are Williston Academy, Deerfield Academy, Northfield-Mount Hermon School, and Stoneleigh-Burnham.

As the river passes the historic town of Deerfield, it picks up the Deerfield River and then Millers River. It continues past the towns of Hatfield, Hadley, and Sunderland, which lie in the heart of the Massachusetts section of the river valley's tobacco belt. Tobacco and onions made these towns prosperous in Colonial days; more recently, plants and flowers, asparagus, apples, strawberries, and raspberries have become significant crops.

At South Hadley, the river is flanked on the east by Mount Holyoke (of 954 feet) and on the west by Mount Tom (1,214 feet). Between them is the Great Oxbow, the subject of a great many paintings. At this point the river passes dinosaur tracks in a quarry and more tracks just south of Mount Tom.

The river is not at its best in the southern half of the Massachusetts reach, as Hampden County is heavily industrialized in the Holyoke, Chicopee, and Springfield areas. And yet, Springfield has a number of firsts to its credit. It was here that Noah Webster's first dictionary was printed, and basketball and one version of the automobile were invented. At this point the volume of water coming from the upper river is considerably augmented by the confluence of the Westfield River flowing from the Berkshires and the Chicopee River from the east. The river widens to its greatest girth of 2,100 feet at Longmeadow.

The river then enters Connecticut, which it divides into two almost equal parts. It passes through rich farmland until it reaches the dams and rapids of Enfield Falls at Windsor Locks. Windsor Locks stands at the head of the tidewater navigation of the river just below the Enfield Dam. The town was settled very early because river cargoes had to be trans-

14

An engraving done in the 1850s shows the panorama of the river valley as seen from the summit of Mount Tom. This view has fascinated a host of writers and painters. Timothy Dwight, in his *Travels in New-England and New-York*, wrote eloquently of its unique beauty, as did his nephew Theodore, Ralph Waldo Emerson, Nathaniel Hawthorne, James Fenimore Cooper, Nathaniel Parker Willis, and Oliver Wendell Holmes, among others. The view of the Oxbow was immortalized by Thomas Cole in his famous painting in 1836, now in New York's Metropolitan Museum. Other artists inspired by this beautiful scenery included William Henry Bartlett, Frederick E. Church, Thomas Charles Farrer, and David John Gue.

Long before interstate turnpike bridges were built over the river, Springfield, Massachusetts, could boast of its impressive and monumental Hampden County Memorial Bridge built in 1923. In the background is the Springfield Campanile, a 300-foot-high bell tower.

ferred by land around the rapids. Across from Windsor Locks is Warehouse Point where William Pynchon, back in 1636, established a warehouse for the cargoes awaiting transfer. The Farmington River joins the Connecticut at Windsor.

The Connecticut River forms a boundary of Hartford, the capital city of Connecticut, where constitutional government as we know it began in 1639 with the promulgation of the Fundamental Orders. After the historic towns of Wethersfield and Glastonbury, the river passes the Dinosaur State Park where over 1,000 prehistoric footprints can be seen in sedimen-

15

The skyline of Hartford, seen from the eastern side of the river, is
unusual for its variety of different and equally distinctive buildings.
In the background can be seen the Morgan Bulkeley Bridge built in
1908, at the time, one of the largest and most beautiful multi-span
stone bridges in the United States.

tary sandstone and fossils. The footprints were discovered as recently as
1966 by a bulldozer operator during the construction of a state highway.

From Rocky Hill, the river is flanked by Cromwell, once known as
Upper Houses, and Portland, the former site of important shipyards and
brownstone quarries, before it reaches Middletown. Middletown is the
home of Wesleyan University and many important industries. Here, the
river takes a southeasterly turn through a narrow valley in the eastern
upland, while the broad, fertile river valley extends from Middletown
down to New Haven. In prehistoric times the river emptied into the sea at
the present site of New Haven. Over the course of time the deposit of
rocks and sandstone forced the waters to the east, thus cutting a new channel for the river through the eastern highlands from Middletown to the
sound.

At the Haddams, the river is joined by the Salmon River and over-
looked by the Connecticut Yankee Nuclear Plant. Wooded hillsides now
line the river as it continues past East Haddam and Chester. The Chester-
Hadlyme Ferry provides a five-minute crossing of the river, hardly time
enough to appreciate the spectacular view up and down the river and the
view of Gillette Castle, which stands 200 feet up on a high cliff in
Hadlyme on the southernmost series called the Seven Sisters. The ferry
has been in continual operation since 1769.

The river flows through loftly rock ledges and the heavily wooded
hillsides of Lyme and Deep River. On the eastern bank is Hamburg Cove
with its beautiful sheltered harbor. On the western bank is Essex, with its

The Chester-Hadlyme Ferry, established in 1769,
is one of two ferries on the river today.

beautiful harbor, narrow streets, fine old houses, and maritime traditions which have given it a character and charm so often associated with the typical New England village. The Connecticut broadens into numerous coves and tidal marshlands, and finally flows into the Long Island Sound between Old Saybrook and Old Lyme. Connecticut has an extensive shoreline of some 250 miles, and none of it actually boarders on the Atlantic. The river flows into the sound some thirty miles west of Montauk Point, Long Island's eastern extremity.

The mouth of the Connecticut, as it is approached from the sound, is a broad estuary a mile in width, made shallow by a large sandbar; a wary navigator must confine his course to the narrow but well-marked channels on the western, or Old Saybrook, side. The sandbar so impeded river navigation by deep draft ships that no industrial development has ever occurred along the shores of the river's mouth. Thus, it has remained in its

The river pours into the Long Island Sound at Old Saybrook. The
Long Jetty, built in the middle of the last century, marks the western
side of the narrow channel from the Sound into the river circumventing the large sandbar in the mile-wide estuary. The outer lighthouse dates from 1866. The inner lighthouse at Lynde Point was
built in 1839 replacing an earlier one established in 1803.

pristine state and, in this respect, is almost unique among the major rivers
of the United States.

In the course of its 410-mile, southward journey, the river falls 1,600
feet. Between its source and the Passumpsic River at Barnet, Vermont, the
descent is 1,200 feet over 132 miles: to Bellows Falls, 105 miles lower, the
descent is 100 feet; for the next fifty-seven miles to Deerfield, it is 160
feet; for the seventy-five miles from Springfield to the sound, the fall is
forty feet. In area, the river basin drains 11,260 square miles, representing
roughly one-third of New Hampshire, Massachusetts, and Connecticut,
and a slightly larger fraction of Vermont.

Although the Connecticut River passes by or through four different
states, its history may well be told as a unit because it has served to inte-
grate the entire valley area. The first settlements along its banks were in
Connecticut, and the next were in lower Massachusetts. Northern Massachusetts, New Hampshire, and Vermont were settled by people emigrating from Connecticut, who brought with them the same Puritan ethic that
had governed them there. Thus, the entire Connecticut River valley was
the site of a very homogeneous population for many years.

2

THE SETTLEMENT OF THE VALLEY

Accordingly in the month of *June*, 1636, they removed an hundred
miles to the westward, with a purpose to settle upon the delightful
banks of *Connecticut River:* and there were about an hundred persons
in the first company that made this removal; who not being able to
walk above ten miles a day took up near a fortnight in the journey;
having no pillows to take their nightly rest upon, but such as their
father *Jacob* found in the way to *Padan-Aram*. Here Mr. *Hooker* was
the chief instrument of beginning another colony . . .

Cotton Mather

The "delightful banks" of the Connecticut River were discovered by a
Dutch sea captain, Adriaen Block, in 1614. Ever since Henry Hudson had
opened up the New York Bay in 1609, the Dutch had been involved in
extensive explorations around the bay area. They had no interest in making permanent settlements; instead, they wanted to establish lucrative
Indian trading posts.

Block was hired by a group of Amsterdam merchants to explore the
area further and bring back valuable furs. He had completed his mission
when his ship, the *Tiger*, burned to the water level. Block enlisted
friendly Indians on Manhattan Island to help him and his crew build a
new ship during the winter.

This vessel, the *Onrust* (meaning "restless"), forty-four and one-half
feet in length, eleven and one-half feet wide, was launched in the spring
of 1614. Thus, having an opportunity for further explorations, Block entered Long Island Sound and sailed up the shore. He passed the Housa-
tonic River and then reached the Connecticut River, which he decided to
explore.

Circumventing the sandbar at the mouth and noting that the river was
"very shallow," Block sailed up the river to the area of Middletown today
where he found some Indian settlements. Proceeding farther upstream to
what is presently South Windsor, he found a village of the Podunk Indians
which had been fortified for defense against the Pequot Indians. (Some
years previously, the Pequots had been driven out of their Hudson River
territory by the Mohawks and had come to Connecticut where they seized
lands of other tribes, so they were regarded as the common enemy.)

Block landed at this village and had a "parley" with the natives who
were very friendly and told him of the fine furs which were to be found in
the river valley. Block then continued up the river to the head of the tidewater at the rapids, now called Enfield Falls. He turned around there,
returned to the sound, and continued along the northern shore to the

Thames River and then to the island we now know as Block Island. Curiously, the island, which had been discovered by Verrazano some one hundred years earlier, is the only site in the entire area to bear Block's name.

Late that summer, Block returned to Amsterdam where he reported to his sponsors on his discoveries and on the great possibilities for fur trading. The area, he added, was "inhabited only by aboriginal savage tribes" and was "unoccupied by any Christian prince or state." The merchants soon sent a number of ships into the area to cultivate the Indian trade.

The following year the merchants received a charter from the Staats-General (the legislature of the Dutch Republic), covering the lands between Virginia and Nova Scotia to be known as New Netherlands. They paid no attention to the English claims to the area which had been asserted since the voyages of the Cabots more than a hundred years earlier. The Dutch were satisfied to simply trade with the Indians for the next few years until, in 1624, they settled New Amsterdam (now New York). Then they established a trading post at the mouth of the Connecticut River, naming it Kievit's Hoek, but this was soon abandoned.

In 1627, the Dutch made overtures to the English Pilgrim group in Plymouth, Massachusetts, for a joint commercial venture in the Connecticut valley. When they failed to reach any agreement with the English, the Dutch acquired some lands from the Indians in the area later known as Hartford and, in 1633, erected a fort and trading post there, calling it the House of (Good) Hope.

In the meantime, a group of Indians from the river valley visited the Plymouth Pilgrims to urge them to come to Connecticut, hoping to secure their protection from the Pequots. They described the land as rich and fertile and abounding in fish, game, and furs. In the summer of 1632, Plymouth's governor, Edward Winslow, sailed up the river in an exploratory trip. The next year he tried to induce the Massachusetts Bay Colony's governor, John Winthrop, to join in the establishment of a trading post along the Connecticut. Winthrop declined, and he gave his reasons in his journal:

> Winthrop's. [July 12, 1633.] Mr. Edward Winslow, governor of Plimouth, and Mr. Bradford came into the bay, and went away the 18th. They came partly to confer about joining in a trade to Connecticut for beaver and hemp. There was a motion to set up a trading house there to prevent the Dutch, who were about to build one; but in regard the place was not fit for plantation, there being three or four thousand warlike Indians, and the river not to be gone into but by smaller pinnaces, having a bar affording but six feet at high water, and for that no vessels can get in for seven months in the year, partly by reason of the ice, and then the violent stream etc., we thought not fit to meddle . . . .

That year, William Holmes, also of Plymouth, sailed up the Connecticut River past the House of Hope with his company. They arrived at the present site of Windsor, where they purchased some land from the Indians and quickly erected a house frame which they had brought with them. They surrounded the house with a stockade as a protection against both the Indians and the Dutch. One month later, some Dutch soldiers came to drive him out, demanding that Holmes "depart forthwith, with all his people and houses." Holmes refused, and the Dutch withdrew without a fight. Further protests from the Dutch were ignored.

Governor Winthrop's lack of interest in the river valley was short-lived. Shortly after his conference with Winslow, his *Blessing of the Bay* (the first ship built in Massachusetts) briefly explored the river. The *Blessing* then proceeded to New Amsterdam to carry Winthrop's remonstration with the Dutch for their settlement on the river, saying that "the King of England had granted the river and country of the Connecticut to his own subjects." The Dutch pointed out that they had been granted these lands by the Staats-General, and each group stood its ground.

Meanwhile, John Oldham, an explorer from Massachusetts Bay, had taken an overland expedition to the river valley and brought back favorable reports on prospective settlements. He returned in 1634 with ten people and settled at the area known today as Wethersfield. In 1635, a considerably larger group migrated overland from the Bay Colony. Some people joined Oldham's and Holmes' groups, and some settled near the House of Hope. They named their settlements Dorchester, Watertown, and Newtown after the settlements from which they had come, but two years later changed the names to Windsor, Wethersfield, and Hartford after their hometowns in England. (In naming Hartford, they misspelled the name of the town of Hereford, which lies near the Welsh border.)

Over the years there have been conflicting arguments as to which town was settled first. Around 1650, the General Court, dominated by the Massachusetts Bay group, stated that Wethersfield was "the most Ancient Towne" on the river, ignoring the 1633 settlement of Windsor by the Plymouth group. The Wethersfield proponents have always claimed that the Windsor settlement and the Dutch settlement at Hartford were merely trading posts, while their town had the first permanent colonists. The Windsor proponents, of course, dispute this claim, and the argument still goes on today.

These settlements barely survived the first recorded hurricane of 1635 and the bitter winter which followed. As told by John Warner Barber in *Connecticut Historical Collections* some two hundred years later:

> By the 15th of November, Connecticut river was frozen over, and the snow was so deep, and the weather so tempestuous, that a considerable number of the cattle could not be brought across the river. The severity of the season was such, and so little time to prepare their huts and shelters for their cattle, that the sufferings of man and beast were extreme. They had shipped their household furniture, and most of their provisions at Boston, but by reason of delays, and the tempestuousness of the season, were either cast away or did not arrive in season.
>
> About the beginning of December, provisions generally failed in the settlements on the river, and famine and death looked the inhabitants in the face. In their distress, some of them in this severe season attempted to go through the wilderness, to the nearest settlement in Massachusetts. A company of thirteen, who made the attempt, lost one of their number, who, in passing a river, fell through the ice and was drowned. The other twelve were ten days on their journey, and had they not received assistance from the Indians, would all have perished. Such was the general distress by the 3d and 4th of December, that a considerable part of the settlers were obliged to leave their habitations. Seventy persons, men, women and children, were obliged in the severity of winter, to go down to the mouth of the river to meet their provisions, as the only expedient to preserve their lives. Not meeting the vessels which they expected, they all went on board of the

Rebecca, a vessel of about 60 tons. This vessel, two days before, was frozen in, twenty miles up the river; but by the falling of a small rain, and the influence of the tide, the ice became so broken, that she made a shift to get out.

She however ran upon the bar, and the people were forced to unlade her to get her off. She was reladed, and in five days reached Boston. Had it not been for these providential circumstances, the people must have perished from famine.

The people who remained and kept their stations on the river, suffered in an extreme degree. After all the help they were able to obtain, by hunting and from the Indians, they were obliged to subsist on acorns, malt and grains. The cattle, which could not be got over the river before winter, lived by browsing in the woods and meadows. They wintered as well, or better, than those that were brought over, and for which all the provision was made, and care taken, of which the settlers were capable.

The year 1635 also saw the building of an English fort at the mouth of the river. In 1620, a group of Puritan noblemen in England had secured the so-called Warwick patent from James I. They had passed the Connecticut part of the grant to another group of Puritans which included Lord Say and Sele, Lord Brook, and Colonel George Fenwick. These gentlemen

Frederick Edwin Church: *Hooker and Company Journeying through the Wilderness to Hartford, 1636.* 1846. The Wadsworth Atheneum. In the words of Connecticut historian, Benjamin Trumbull, they "travelled more than a hundred miles, through a hideous and trackless wilderness, to Hartford. They had no guide but their compass; made their way over mountains, through swamps, thickets, and rivers, which were not passable but with great difficulty. They had no cover but the heavens, nor any lodgings but those which simple nature afforded them. They drove with them a hundred and sixty head of cattle, and by the way, subsisted on the milk of their cows. Mrs. Hooker was borne through the wilderness upon a litter. The people generally carried their packs, arms, and some utensils. They were nearly a fortnight on their journey."

planned to establish a settlement in Connecticut where Puritan noblemen and gentry might find refuge from both the royal absolutism of the Stuarts and the religious domination of the established Anglican Church. So, in 1635, they commissioned John Winthrop, Jr., son of the governor of the Massachusetts Bay Colony, to establish a new colony at the mouth of the river (which was still being claimed by the Dutch), and this transpired under the command of Lieutenant Lion Gardiner. The settlement was named Say-Brook, in honor of the two leading proprietors.

The following year, Reverend Thomas Hooker and William Pynchon led their families and friends out of the Massachusetts Bay Colony. Both men had grown restless under the theocratic oligarchy of the bay's John Cotton. Hooker's group settled in Hartford, and Pynchon's group went to Agawam, later known as Springfield.

With his establishment of Springfield, Pynchon also received certain exclusive trading rights with the Indians, and he quickly set up a systematic river business. He noted that about halfway between Springfield and Hartford was the head of tidewater at the Enfield Falls. Cargoes had to be carried around the falls and then reloaded on flat boats or rafts to continue on their way. A few miles below the falls, therefore, Pynchon built a warehouse for the storage of merchandise awaiting shipment by boat up or down the river. This site has since been known as Warehouse Point and remained as the place of transshipment of freight until the early years of the nineteenth century.

More Connecticut settlements followed. In 1638, a separate colony was established at New Haven by John Davenport, a dissident Puritan divine, and Theophilus Eaton, a prosperous merchant who came from England initially to settle in Massachusetts but who chose to proceed farther to the west. A year later, this group branched out to Guilford, Branford, Milford, and Stamford. The year 1640 saw the foundation of New London by the same John Winthrop, Jr., of the Saybrook group.

It is not always appreciated that the leaders of the first Puritan settlements in New England were men of considerable educational, cultural, and even financial background who, out of their strong religious convictions, braved the rigors, hardships, and uncertainties of the wilderness to establish wholly new communities thousands of miles from their homeland. Thomas Hooker and John Cotton had come from Emmanuel College in Cambridge, the so-called mother house of Puritanism; John Davenport came from Magdalen College in Oxford; John Winthrop, Sr., from Trinity College in Cambridge, was a prosperous lawyer in England before coming to Massachusetts; his son, John Jr., went to Trinity College in Dublin and also was a lawyer before he came to Connecticut.

During the years of these early settlements, Connecticut had a comparatively dense concentration of Indians, estimated at six or seven thousand. These were divided into a number of tribes of the Algonquian confederation who were in constant quarrels and fights with each other. They were generally willing, however, to cooperate with the Dutch and English by selling them land or trading furs with them.

The Pequot Indians, on the other hand, were very fierce, so the early English settlements along the river were concentrated in small hamlets behind palisades and fortifications to protect them from Pequot attacks. The settlers had no roads, and Indian trails were obvious hazards, so the

Statue of Lion Gardiner at Saybrook Point.

Lion Gardiner (1599-1663) was an expert military engineer in service in the Netherlands when he married his Dutch wife. He settled Saybrook in 1635 and lived there with his wife. Their son, David, was the first white child born in Connecticut. In 1640, Gardiner left Saybrook and purchased from the Indians an island across the sound which he named Gardiner's Island. He then obtained a royal patent, and the island has remained in his family for some sixteen generations. His son, David, died rather suddenly on a visit to Hartford, and the following epitaph was inscribed over his grave:

"Here lyeth the body of Mr. David Gardiner of Gardiners Island Deceased July 10, 1689 in the fifty fourth year of his age. Well, Sick, Dead in one hours space. Engrave the remembrance of Death on thine Heart When as thou dost see how swiftly hours depart."

river was their only highway. The Pequots hated the exploiting Dutch traders and the English settlers who coveted their lands. It was not long before they were embroiled initially with the Dutch and then with the English. As early as 1634, they massacred a band of English traders under Captain John Stone of Virginia near Joshua's Rock in the lower river. In 1636, they attacked and killed John Oldham near Block Island. The next year they attacked Wethersfield, killed nine men, and carried off two girls, who were later rescued by the Dutch.

The settlers now retaliated, realizing that some united action between them would be necessary if they were to survive the Pequot attacks. A force was raised in Hartford, Windsor, and Wethersfield, under the command of Captain John Mason, and repaired to Saybrook to serve under the leadership of Lion Gardiner. With the help of the Mohicans, the small force pursued the Pequots to a fort in the Mystic area and attacked them at dawn on May 26, 1637.

Most of the Indians were asleep, but they quickly rallied. The English then set the village on fire, shooting any Indians attempting to escape. In the words of Captain Mason:

> When [the fire] was thoroughly kindled the Indians ran as men dreadfully amazed. And indeed such a dreadful Terror did the Almighty let fall upon their Spirits that they would fly from us and run into the very flames, where many of them perished. And when the Fort was thoroughly fired, command was given that all should fall off and surround the Fort which was readily attended by all . . .
>
> "Thus were they now at their wits end, who not many hours before exalted themselves in their great pride, threatening and resolving the utter ruin and destruction of all the English, exulting and rejoicing with songs and dances. But God was above them, who laughed his enemies and the enemies of His People to scorn, making them as a

Statue of Thomas Hooker in front of Old State House in Hartford.

Thomas Hooker (1586-1647) fled to Holland in 1630 after being charged in England with non-conformist preaching. In 1633, he migrated to Massachusetts where he became pastor of the Newtown (Cambridge) church. He disputed with John Cotton, the leading minister of the Bay Colony, over the role of the clergy in the community, and led his followers overland to Hartford. Here he promulgated the Fundamental Orders which were to be a cornerstone in the development of American law. Hooker died in Hartford in 1647. As there is no existing likeness of Hooker, this 1950 statue by Frances Wadsworth represents him as he was believed to have appeared.

fiery oven: Thus were the Stout Hearted spoiled, having slept their last sleep and none of their Men could find their Hands: Thus did the Lord judge among the Heathen, filling the Place with dead Bodies! . . . And thus, in little more than one hour's space was their impregnable Fort with themselves utterly destroyed to the number of 600 or 700, as some of themselves confessed. There were only 7 taken captive, and about 7 escaped. Of the English there were 9 slain outright, and about 20 wounded.

After two further defeats, the Pequots were broken and scattered. This was, however, the beginning of animosities between the whites and the Indians which were to culminate in King Philip's War later in the century.

A general court was established to prosecute the Pequot War in 1637 in Hartford. After the dispersal of the Pequots, the court continued as a form of political association, and the Connecticut groups who now considered themselves beyond the jurisdiction of their Massachusetts progenitors formed themselves into a separate commonwealth. They adopted the Fundamental Orders in 1639 which were inspired by a sermon of Thomas Hooker and drafted by Roger Ludlow who had been a member of the Inner Temple of the London Bar. This was the first formal adoption in the American colonies of the principle of self-government based on the popular will, or, in Hooker's words, "The foundation of authority is laid firstly in the free consent of the people." By people, Hooker meant only those who would take the prescribed religious oath and, indeed, for many years the right to vote in Connecticut was in effect limited to church members in good standing.

While the English were expanding their settlements along the sound and up the river, the Dutch continued their trading activities, which

William Pynchon (1590-1662), the founder of Springfield, was a man of great ability and, even more remarkably for early New England, a man of broad tolerance. In the words of Franklin D. Roosevelt on the Springfield tercentenary in 1936:

"William Pynchon was a versatile man. Besides being a successful colonizer, he was, we know, an astute business man, a scholar and a born leader — just the type of man who would lay broad and deep the foundations of a new community. We know also that he was a theologian whose controversial book on the Atonement, anticipating the conclusions of later liberal theologians, was, by order of the General Court, publicly burned in the Market Place of Boston. Surely a man who touched life at so many angles as William Pynchon deserves to be remembered."

brought them into confrontation with the English. In 1639, the Director General of New Amsterdam, William Kieft, sent the well-known Dutch navigator, David DeVries, on a diplomatic mission to the English Governor in Hartford in an endeavor to reconcile the conflicting territorial claims of the English and the Dutch over the area.

First, DeVries arrived at Saybrook on June 7th, where he was received by Lion Gardiner and his wife. After a pleasant visit with Gardiner, who had seen service in Holland as an engineer on the staff of the Prince of Orange, DeVries took leave and proceeded up the river. DeVries noted in his log: "The river is a pleasant, beautiful river, where many thousands of Christians could flourish by farming and they should be helped to do so," an interesting comment in light of the abysmal failure of the Dutch West India Company to consider its North American outposts as anything beyond mere trading centers.

When DeVries arrived at the House of Hope, he found a small, poorly equipped outpost, manned by fifteen soldiers. Inside the compound was a blockhouse, a two-story building about twenty-six feet in length with a large central building. There was also a small pasture for hogs, cattle, horses, and poultry. Outside the stockade, DeVries wrote, "is a farm, containing a kitchen garden with beans, pumpkins, and other vegetables, a large field of maize, and a good-sized orchard of apples, cherries, pears, and peaches. There is no chapel, but there is a burying ground with grave markers of sandstone."

In contrast to the small Dutch post, DeVries noted about Hartford that "the English in spite of us have begun to build up a small town and have a fine church and over one hundred houses." DeVries met with Governor John Haynes, but nothing was resolved. The English were adamant in their claims, and it was clear that their intent was to squeeze out the Dutch as soon and as gracefully as possible. It was not long before Dutch indifference and incompetence gave way to the force of numbers and the organizational persistence of the English settlers. War broke out in 1653 between England and Holland, and in 1654, the House of Hope was seized and taken over by the Connecticut colony. Thus it was that the days of the Dutch presence on the river were forever over.

Sometime after DeVries' visit, Colonel George Fenwick arrived in Saybrook with his bride, Lady Alice Fenwick. Saybrook had been founded for Puritan "gentlemen of distinction and qualitie," but Fenwick was the only gentleman of substance who actually settled there. The settlement expanded under Fenwick's direction, and Lady Fenwick was said to have introduced gardening and other amenities into the still rough and primitive living. Unfortunately, several years later, the good lady died in childbirth. She was buried within the settlement, but in 1870 her remains were moved to a cemetery on Saybrook Point.

During Fenwick's years in Saybrook, he was approached by leaders from the other river colonies to discuss a proposed confederation of the colonies, principally for mutual defense against the Indians and, to a lesser extent, against the Dutch. In 1643, Fenwick attended the first meeting of the "United Colonies of New England," and soon thereafter was

Hartford, shown here in 1640, was described in glowing terms by Dutch visitor, David DeVries.

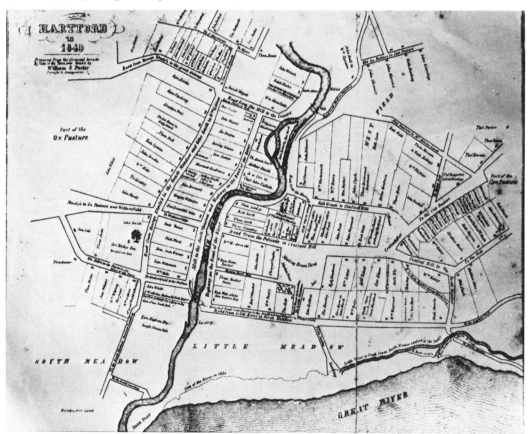

Rev. Thomas Hooker's House.

' The above is a front view of the house of the Rev. Thomas Hooker, (the first minister in Connecticut.) The projection in front (A) was called the porch, and was used as his study. This building stood in School street, on the north side of the high and romantic banks of Mill river. The drawing was taken immediately before it was taken down.

First Meeting House built in Connecticut.

The above is believed to be a correct representation of the first house ever erected in Connecticut for Christian worship. The drawing was obtained from a gentleman now deceased, who devoted considerable time and attention to antiquarian researches in Hartford : the drawing of Mr. Hooker's house was obtained from the same individual.

elected as a Connecticut magistrate. In 1644, Fenwick agreed to let Saybrook become part of the Connecticut colony. The Saybrook settlement was absorbed, or more precisely, bought out for 1600 pounds, and Fenwick transferred all the rights of the patentees under the Warwick patent to the Connecticut colony. Whether the other patentees consented to this transaction is not known but, in any event, Fenwick returned to England, and Saybrook and the other river towns grew and prospered together. (Colonel Fenwick is remembered today in the borough of Fenwick, a private enclave to the south of Old Saybrook, developed after the Civil War by prominent Hartford insurance and manufacturing executives for their summer homes.)

The Connecticut colony was not as successful in retaining Springfield. There had been disagreements for a number of years because of their divergent interests. The Connecticut towns concentrated their efforts on the cultivation of their land and the establishment of a community motivated by Hooker's concepts of theocracy. Pynchon and his family were more interested in the development of profitable trade along the river. Finally, in 1643, when the New England confederation was organized, Springfield joined as part of Massachusetts. Nevertheless, despite the jurisdictional differences, the economic interests of Springfield more closely paralleled those of Connecticut than those around Massachusetts Bay, and the river continued to serve for almost two centuries as a unifying factor of the river towns.

It turned out that there was no real unity in the "United Colonies of New England," which encompassed the Massachusetts, Plymouth, Connecticut, and New Haven colonies. All the colonies still were guaranteed their respective territories and independence, and the confederation accomplished little.

As was to be expected, in their first years the colonists encountered numerous economic problems. There was a shortage of labor. They needed manufactured goods which had to be imported from England through Boston. Payment for the goods was difficult because there were few staples available for export. Bit by bit, however, these problems were overcome and, by the middle of the century, the settlements along the river were on a solid base.

John Warner Barber *Connecticut Historical Collections*, New Haven, 1836. Most houses at the time were very small and simple, but Hooker, as the leader of the colony, had a more elaborate house. It was built shortly after 1636 and was torn down around 1820. Barber reproduced both the house and the meeting house from drawings made by a now unknown antiquarian.

The Buttolph-Williams House, built around 1690 in Wethersfield, is a characteristic late seventeenth century river valley dwelling. The house has been completely restored by the Antiquarian and Landmarks Society of Connecticut. It contains a collection of pewter, delft, fabrics, and furniture of the century, along with a kitchen considered to be the most completely furnished seventeenth century kitchen in New England. In its primitive sternness, the house reflects the stark way of life of the early days. The house was almost destroyed in the hurricane of 1938 when a huge maple fell upon its roof and, for some years, it seriously deteriorated until it was rescued in the nick of time by the Society.

3

THE COLONIES TAKE HOLD

The Lord hath been pleased to turn all the wigwams, hurts, and hovels
the English dwelt in at their first coming, into orderly, fair, and well-
built houses, well furnished many of them, together with Orchards
filled with goodly fruit trees, and gardens with variety of flowers . . .

Edward Johnson

The second half of the seventeenth century saw a measure of prosperity
beginning to come to the river valley. When the settlers first arrived, they
had built very small and simple log houses. These were easy to build and
provided immediate shelter. In time, the colonists began to build more
permanent structures, two-story houses built around a great center chimney with a large fireplace and, in later years, a brick oven. As the house-
holder became more prosperous, he added a lean-to at the rear of the
house to increase the number of rooms. Soon the lean-to became a basic
part of the house, turning it into a saltbox design. The first saltbox houses
were seen in the late years of the century.

The beginning of prosperity was due to the resourcefulness of the
river valley settlers. Agriculture, at first, was their main occupation because it made them self-sufficient. The principal crops were corn, rye,
oats, barley, flax, and hemp, as well as miscellaneous vegetables and
fruits. Tobacco was planted at Windsor in the 1640s, and red onions
thrived around Wethersfield. In the beginning, these crops were grown
for the settlers' use only, while furs and skins were used in trade for other
necessary supplies. Soon, however, the settlers grew more than they
needed so they could trade their surplus crops, plus livestock and forest
products. Most of their trade was with Boston and New York, which could
be reached easily. Boston was the center of the New England trade, so the
river valley settlers had little direct trade with England. Their products
were exchanged in Boston for finished goods coming from England.

The settlers also traded directly with the West Indies, and it was not
long before the building of ships became their highest priority. Shipbuilding became a major activity along the river banks, and soon small
vessels of every description were to be found along the riverfront.

The first vessel to be built along the river for the West Indies trade
was the *Tryall*, built by Thomas Deming at Wethersfield in 1649. It was
followed in 1666 by the ketch *Diligence*, owned by a syndicate headed by
Robert Lay of Potapaug (now Essex). The *Diligence* was a ketch with "one
mainsail, foresail, topsail and mizzen." The noted historian of the Connecticut River, Thomas A. Stevens, tells us that in "November of 1666,

Captain Chester set sail in the *Diligence* from Lay's Wharf, which was on the Connecticut River in front of his house, bound for Barbados in the West Indies. The cargo consisted of horses, hay, peas, Indian corn, bran and candles. His return cargo consisted of 'Good Rum and Sugar.' "

Ship-building was encouraged by the public authorities. In 1666, the Connecticut General Court exempted all vessels on the stocks from taxation. According to Stevens: "By 1680, the Colony of 12,000 people had 27 vessels in seagoing trade, including four ships, three pinks, eight sloops and other vessels totaling 1,050 tons."

Sailboat days on the river were not without their difficulties. The river was unmarked, and shoals were not dredged. Sailing up the river could also be a problem, as the flood tide was not always sufficient to carry the ship upstream against the current. More often than not, the ship had to be pulled by the crew with a rope from ashore or from an anchor dropped upstream.

Some of the vessels found along the riverfront were river ferries. The first ferry was at Windsor in 1641, which was followed by four other ferries on the lower river during the rest of the century. The earliest ferries were canoes, and later ones were flatboats. They were propelled by oars, pushed by long poles from the stern, or pulled across the river with a rope or chain. Fares were regulated by the General Court and were the subject of considerable complaints from both the ferrymen and the public at large.

Thomas Cadwell was a ferryman at Hartford. His agreement with the Court in 1682 provided that he should "keepe the ffery att Hartford . . . at the Common Landing Place . . . and the said Thomas Cadwell is to maintaine a sufficient Boat ffor the passage of Horse and man; and a Connoe . . . to carry over single persons."

During this period, settlements expanded along the river. From Hartford there was a move down the river; Glastonbury, Cromwell, and Middletown were settled around 1650. Haddam followed a dozen years later, with East Haddam being settled about 1680. All of these towns were a part of Hartford County until 1785, when Middlesex County was formed. Middletown and the Haddams were then included in the new county.

In the lower valley, then a part of New London County, the movement was up river from Saybrook. Lyme was settled about 1650 as East Saybrook. It remained a part of Saybrook until it was separately incorporated in 1665 with the signing of an agreement between the two towns known as the "Loving Parting." Matthew Griswold, the first settler in Lyme, named the town for Lyme Regis in Dorsetshire, England, the town Old Lyme, Lyme, East Lyme, part of Hadlyme, and part of Salem. (In 1854, the town of Saybrook became Old Saybrook, leaving Saybrook the name of Deep River until 1947. In 1857, Old Lyme was separated from Lyme.)

In the 1670s there was a longstanding boundary dispute between New London and Lyme about a four-mile wide strip of land, and John Barber, in his *Connecticut Historical Collections*, related how it was solved:

> New London proposed to take three miles in width, and leave one to Lyme. Lyme made a similar proposal to New London. The distance to the seat of government was fifty miles. The journey lay through a wilderness inhabited by savages, and crossed by numerous streams, over

The ferry between Rocky Hill and Glastonbury was established in 1655. It is the oldest continuously operated ferry on the Connecticut River and probably in the United States.

which no bridges were erected. The land, though now of considerable value, was then regarded as a trifling object. The expense of appointing agents to manage the cause before the Legislature was considerable, and the hazard of the journey not small. In this situation, the inhabitants of both townships agreed to settle their respective titles to the land in controversy, by a combat between two champions to be chosen by each for that purpose. New London selected two men by the names of Picket and Latimer. Lyme committed its cause to two others, named Grisold and Ely. On a day mutually appointed, the champions appeared in the field, and fought with their fists, till victory declared in favor of each of the Lyme combatants. Lyme then quietly took possession of the controverted tract, and has held it undisputed to the present day.

Essex, originally known as Potapaug, was settled in 1648 and remained a part of Saybrook until 1852, when it became a separate town, taking the name of Essex two years later. It was followed by what is now Deep River, and then by Chester in 1692.

Upriver from Springfield, settlement was equally rapid in the fertile Pioneer Valley. Northampton was settled about 1653, followed by Hadley a few years later, Deerfield in 1670, Northfield in 1673, and Greenfield in 1686.

Meanwhile, in England, after two civil wars, Charles I had lost his throne and head in 1648. (As a matter of fact, two of his regicides, Edward Whalley and William Goffe, wanted for trial in England after the restoration of the monarchy in 1660, were said to have been hidden in Hadley for some twenty years in the parsonage of John Russell.)

While England was under the leadership of Oliver Cromwell, the Puritans of New England had a sense of security. This feeling of comfort, however, did not last long, and the Restoration in 1660, with the crowning of Charles II, came as a shock to the New England colonies. Nevertheless, representatives of the Connecticut colony met in Hartford and pledged loyalty to the new king. The colony was under the governorship of John Winthrop, Jr., and the general court in Hartford entrusted him with the mission of petitioning the king for a new charter.

In this mission, Winthrop, one of the most talented of the early colonists, was eminently successful, and in 1662, Connecticut was granted a royal charter. The boundaries of Connecticut were established, and it was to be governed by an elected governor, with an elective council and assembly chosen, albeit, from a limited group of male churchgoers with additional qualifications of land tenure. The charter encompassed substantially all of present-day Connecticut. Initially, it was resisted by the New Haven colony, but within a few years the New Haven towns were gradually absorbed.

Winthrop's achievement was extraordinary. By his own savvy and with his ability to enlist support from various groups around the crown, he, son of the first Puritan governor of Massachusetts and representing a thoroughly Puritan constituency, managed to obtain from the son of the king executed by the Puritans a charter which gave Connecticut citizens greater·liberties and freedom than any other colony and, indeed, greater than those of Englishmen in Britain itself. This charter was to endure as fundamental law in Connecticut for over 150 years.

Under the Connecticut charter, the colony was self governing. The assembly consisted of a council and a house of representatives. The gover-

The Connecticut Charter was obtained in 1662 by John Winthrop, Jr. from Charles II, whose likeness appears on the upper left-hand side.

John Winthrop, Jr. (1606-1676) had been recognized as titular governor of the Connecticut Colony in 1636, and was elected as governor in 1657 and annually thereafter from 1659 to 1676. He was also a promoter of scientific studies, and in 1663 was the first colonist to be elected as a fellow of the Royal Society in London. His father was governor of Massachusetts Bay Colony, and his son, Fitz-John Winthrop, served as governor from 1698 to 1707. Thus, three generations of Winthrops served as governors of Massachusetts or Connecticut over a period of almost eighty years.

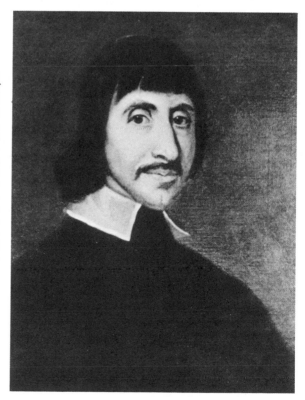

nor elected by the eligible voters was, in fact, subservient to the assembly. Political contacts with London were avoided as much as possible, and various attempts on the part of certain British interests to revoke the charter came to naught. Connecticut was probably the most independent of all the British colonies in America.

Massachusetts was governed under the 1629 charter granted to the "Governor and Company of the Massachusetts Bay in New England" which also provided for a large degree of home rule.

In both Connecticut and Massachusetts, each town was politically and economically an entity unto itself. Government was by town meeting where any citizen could freely voice his opinion. The voters elected the town officials and established ordinances and procedures for the town meetings which were concerned with every aspect of town activities. In the older settlements of Hartford, Windsor, and Wethersfield, the records reflect the following concerns: the order of the conduct of divine services, the punishment of misbehaving youths, the renting of premises to strangers, the providing of wood and provisions for the infirm elderly, the draining of turpentine from the pine trees (which was a valuable fuel for lighting purposes), the appointment of teachers, ministers, and their salaries — usually paid in kind — awards for the killing of wolves, mandates upon the citizens to kill a quota of blackbirds, and more.

The people in Connecticut were ruled by a revised codification of Roger Ludlow's laws, which had been adopted in 1650. The importance of protecting individual rights was stressed in the preamble:

> . . . no mans life shall bee taken away, no mans honor or good name shall bee stained, no mans person shall be arrested, restrained, banished, dismembered nor any way punnished; no man shall bee deprived of his wife or children, no mans goods or estate shall bee taken away from him, nor any wayes indamaged, vnder colour of Law . . . vnless it bee by the vertue or equity of some express Law of the Country warranting the same, established by a Generall Courte, and sufficiently published, or in case of the defect of a Law in any perticular case, by the word of God.

The provisions of the code reflected many of the pressing problems of the times. The defense of the settlements was important. All persons above the age of sixteen years, except magistrates and church officers, were required to bear arms with ammunition. Intercourse with the Indians was strictly limited. Children were required to "Read the Inglish tounge" and to be trained in husbandry. Education was to be encouraged. Excessive drinking was a problem:

> And euery person found drunken, viz: so that hee bee thereby . . . dissabled in the vse of his vnderstanding, appearing in his speech or gesture, in any of the saide howses or elsewhere, shall forfeitt ten shillings; and for excessiue drinking, three shillings, foure pence; and for continnuing aboue halfe an houre tipling, two shillings six pence; and for tipling at vnseasonable times, or after nine a clock at night, fiue shillings . . . and for want of payment, such shall bee imprisoned vntill they pay, or bee set in the stocks, one houre or more, in some open place, as the weather will permitt, not exceeding three houres at one time . . .

Church attendance was required, and fines were imposed for not observing the Sabbath and for interrupting the preacher. The death penalty was prescribed for fourteen crimes including not only murder, but also witchcraft, blasphemy, unchastity, cursing, insulting parents, and incorrigible stubbornness on the part of children.

Indeed, the first execution for witchcraft in New England took place in Hartford, in 1647, thirty-five years before the Salem trials of Massachusetts. A year later, a Wethersfield woman was arrested, and a "Bill of Inditement" was brought against her accusing her of "familiarity with the Deuill." She was executed in Hartford, and Increase Mather reported that "She dyd in a frame extreamly to the satisfaction of them that were spectators of it." In 1651, a Wethersfield carpenter and his wife were indicted for having "Interteined familiarity with Sathan, the Greate Enemye of God and Mankinde," and they were hanged two years later. Springfield records show that one woman was hanged in 1651. All in all, eleven people in the river valley lost their lives during the witchcraft craze which lasted from 1647 to 1670, far fewer than the twenty who perished in the Salem witch hunts.

There was little joy of life in the valley towns in these times. Music, except for a few old folk songs and the five psalm tunes tolerated in the church, was nonexistent. There were no theaters nor public entertainment, no dancing, little painting, no sculpture, and no literature except for long-winded sermons and a few interesting diaries. This environment, coupled with the Puritan ethic, resulted in strict living, and it was no accident that Connecticut was called the "land of steady habits," fundamentalist in religion and conservative in public affairs. The people were convinced their ways of life reflected the will of God in all their activities.

Puritan life was indeed centered around the stern God and the earthly family. Over the latter, the father held absolute authority as the deputy of the Lord. The wife's position was that of housekeeper and mother. Married at age sixteen or seventeen, young wives brought forth children in rapid succession. It was not unusual for a young wife to die in childbirth after bearing seven or eight children. Most husbands then remarried and lessened their demands for progeny.

Family discipline was strict, and the law required that the father instruct his children in "an honest calling" or a "profitable trade." One of the boys would probably follow in the trade of the father, and others would in due course be apprenticed to a friend or neighbor in a different trade. The future of girls was limited to motherhood and housework.

An important occupation of the household was the making of cloth. Wives, children, and grandparents were involved in winding the quills and turning the reels so as to accomplish the unending work at the loom or spinning wheel.

The principal meal was served at noon with Indian meal pudding, boiled beef, pork, or fish. Fish was so abundant along the river shores that apprentices, in signing up for study and keep, would stipulate that salmon would be served no more than twice a week. (In those days, shad was considered as fit for only the very poor or for use as fertilizer.) With the abundance of berries, apples, plums, and other fruits, the Puritan wife soon excelled in the making of pies, tarts, and other pastries.

The level of education was unusually high. According to the law, local authorities were to work with parents so as "not to suffer so much barbarism in any of the families as to have a single child or apprentice unable to read the holy word of God, and the good laws of the colony." Initially, each town of fifty families was required to maintain a school, and in 1658, the requirement was reduced to thirty families.

The prevailing religion throughout the river valley was Congregational, and every settlement had a meetinghouse on the green which served as a church, town hall, and community center. Originally a severe rectangular structure, it was not until over one hundred years later that the meetinghouse came to be called a "church" when the building was painted, a steeple was added, and singing, silver, and flowers were introduced. The schoolhouse was close to the meetinghouse, as were the parsonage, general store, and offices, in some cases for the lawyer and doctor.

The Congregational minister of the gospel was one of the community leaders and frequently served as schoolmaster. Church and state were united, and the church was supported by public taxation. Dissent was not tolerated, and in Connecticut, at least, creeds professing other than the Congregational faith were subject to repressive measures.

During these years, there were few problems with the Indians, mainly because of the continuing alliance between the river colonists and the Mohegans under the leadership of Uncas. The situation was not so peaceful in coastal Massachusetts where the Indians were being subjected to increasing pressures from the colonists who coveted their lands and threatened their sovereignty. After a number of skirmishes, the Wam-

August Saint-Gaudens' statue of Deacon Samuel Chapin, better known as "The Puritan," epitomizes in stone the character of the Connecticut Valley Puritan. It stands at the head of the Springfield Quadrangle. The background is the tower of Christ Church Cathedral.

panoags, under their leader "King Philip," and the Narragansetts, under Canonchet, formed a coalition and began a series of assaults on eastern Massachusetts and Rhode Island.

At first, the Indian raids were confined to the Narragansett country, but in 1675, they spread to the upper valley where Deerfield and Northfield had been recently established as the northernmost frontier settlements of the Massachusetts Bay Colony. These settlements consisted of a log hut and a primitive meetinghouse surrounded by stockades. When the Indian attacks began, the colonists took refuge behind the stockades until they could be rescued. After many skirmishes and ambushes, the settlers were finally evacuated, and the Indians burned the settlements.

In contrast to the Pequot War where the Indians fought with bows, arrows, and tomahawks, King Philip's Indians were equipped with firearms. Cruelty was rampant on both sides. At Northfield, the Indians set the heads of dead soldiers on poles along the roadside. At Springfield, an Indian squaw was ordered to be "tourne in peeces by dogs & shee was so delt withall." At Hatfield, an English soldier was put to death after the Indians "burnt his nails, put his feet tscald against the fire, and drove a stake through one of his feet to pin him to the ground."

After several setbacks, the colonists in the upper river valley, Rhode Island, and around Plymouth were able to isolate groups of Indians and defeat them piecemeal. Canonchet was captured and executed in April, 1676, and his head was sent to Hartford. Philip was killed in August, and his body was drawn and quartered. His head was displayed on a pole in Plymouth.

The war lasted until 1676 and was extremely costly to the colonists. A number of towns were destroyed and homes burned. Nearly every family had a member who had been injured or killed. At long last, however, the Indians were virtually exterminated in southern New England and thereafter were no longer a force to be reckoned with.

While Connecticut was making a substantial contribution to the struggle against the Indians, a new and different threat appeared in the person of Sir Edmund Andros. In 1674, Andros had been appointed governor of the Province of New York by the Duke of York, the brother of Charles II, who later became James II. Notwithstanding the grant of the 1662 Winthrop charter, Charles had subsequently granted the New York province to his brother, including in the grant "all of the land from the west side of the Connecticut River to the east side of Delaware Bay." In 1675, Andros asked for the land west of the river, and when Connecticut did not comply, he appeared off Saybrook with a small fleet and demanded the surrender of the land. When the local militia threatened armed resistance, Andros found discretion the better part of valor and quietly withdrew, but he was to return later.

The last years of Charles' reign saw a trend toward the consolidation of the New England colonies into one governmental unit. The accession of James II in 1685 brought with it the creation of the Dominion of New England and the revocation of the Massachusetts charter. In 1686, Andros became royal governor of New England and promptly set about to obtain the submission of Connecticut. In October, 1687, he arrived in Hartford where he was officially and politely received by the authorities. Legend has it that, on the last day of his visit, he demanded the surrender of the

charter. While the matter was being discussed, the lights were extin-
guished, and the charter disappeared. Reportedly it had been carried off
by one Captain Wadsworth and hidden in a large hollow tree in front of
the house of Samuel Wyllys, a magistrate of the colony. (The tree, to be
known as the great Charter Oak, blew down in a storm in 1856. At that time
it was 33 feet in circumference, and its wood was used for many pieces of
furniture which are now in museums and private collections. A tablet
marks the spot where the tree stood, and the story of the Charter Oak
remains as one of Connecticut's best-loved traditions.)

Notwithstanding the disappearance of the charter, Andros took over
the rule of the colony, annexing it to Massachusetts. The new regime,
however, was short-lived. A little over a year later, James II was over-
thrown in the so-called "Glorious Revolution"; Andros was arrested in
Boston and returned to England, and Connecticut was re-established as a
separate colony under the 1662 charter. Massachusetts did not fare so well
and continued as a royal province.

By the end of the century the Connecticut colony had grown to a population of about 30,000. The population of the Massachusetts river towns
was probably around 3,000. The settlement of the valley of the Connecticut River in New Hampshire and in what was later to become Vermont
would not take place until the second quarter of the eighteenth century.

Sir Edmund Andros (1637-1714)
has always been thought a *bête
noire* in American history, but, although overbearing and high-
handed, he was an efficient
administrator. Prior to his service
in New England, he had been governor of New York (1674-1681). After his return to England, he
returned to the Colonies as governor of Virginia until 1697.

4

WAR AND PEACE

... the awful work of that expedition, in the burning of the town, the massacre or capture of nearly all its inhabitants, and the marching of one hundred and twelve captives, the minister with his flock, three hundred miles over the ice and snow to Canada ... has become familiar in history and legend as 'The Sack of Deerfield.'

Edwin M. Bacon
The Connecticut River

The end of the seventeenth century and the beginning of the eighteenth was a time of war and peace along the upper river, and peace and prosperity along the lower river in Connecticut. The Indians were no longer a threat in Connecticut, so the colonists could concentrate on the growth of commerce and shipping and on the improvement of their way of life.

Along the upper river, however, the Indians were allied with the French and engaged in numerous conflicts with the English and the settlers. These confrontations were but small reflections of the unending duel between Great Britain and France for what in those years amounted to world hegemony. The British and French clashed not only in their North American colonies, but also in their colonies in the West Indies and India, as well as in a good part of western Europe. The problem in North America was that the French had settled in Canada, then called New France, and wanted to keep the British from expanding their settlements farther north along the Connecticut River. Thus, there were frequent raids and skirmishes all along the boundary between British North America and New France.

The first conflict was King William's War, from 1689 to 1697, during which the towns in the upper river valley suffered through a series of raids and attacks. One such town was the British outpost of Deerfield, which had been rebuilt after being burned in King Philip's War. Once again Deerfield bore the brunt of several raids by the Indians, aided and abetted by their French allies.

Even more serious was Queen Anne's War, from 1702 to 1713. In Europe, this was known as the War of Spanish Succession, which culminated in the emergence of Great Britain as the world's greatest sea power. The immediate effect of the struggle in the upper river valley was a series of border raids by the French and Indians, the most famous of which centered in Deerfield.

Early in 1704, the French governor of Canada sent out a force of French and Indians to destroy this settlement which then had a population of 268 people living in forty-one homes. On February twenty-nine,

The Frary house in Deerfield dates from 1740. Historic Deerfield has over thirty buildings more than 150 years old. In many of these buildings, varying modes of life are depicted from the early eighteenth century settlers to the time of the more prosperous merchants and land owners.

Deerfield was taken by surprise by the French-Indian force. Forty-nine were killed, and 112 were captured. The town was burned, and the captured, including women, children and infants, were marched through the snow-filled woods and hills and across icy streams to Montreal. Twenty-one prisoners perished on the trek north. This ordeal was memorialized in the account of the Reverend John Williams who, along with most of the survivors, was eventually ransomed and returned to Deerfield.

The end of Queen Anne's War brought about almost a generation of peace. Trade was expanded, and the upper valley became an important source of ship timber for the rapidly growing royal navy. There was considerable migration to the upper valley from Connecticut and Massachusetts, as well as from abroad. Settlement initially took the form of forts and outposts designed to protect the lower settlements from possible French and Indian raids. Fort Dummer, which was established in 1724 near what is now Brattleboro, was the first permanent settlement in what would become Vermont, and the northernmost outpost. The fort was under the command of Captain Timothy Dwight. Dwight lived there with his wife, and their son was born at the fort, the first white child to be born in Vermont.

Other outposts were later established. One was built in Bellows Falls in 1735; a year later Walpole and Charlestown on the east side of the river and Rockingham and Westminster on the west side were settled. Further outposts later were established to the north, but jurisdictional disputes arose between Massachusetts and New Hampshire because both claimed the area. This conflict was eventually settled in 1740 by King George II in favor of New Hampshire, restricting Massachusetts to the area it occupies today.

The next year New Hampshire received its own royal governor, Benning Wentworth, whose commission defined the New Hampshire territory as running "due West Cross the said river (Merrimack) till it meets with our other Governments." Wentworth governed New Hampshire for twenty-five years from his oceanside house until his greediness caused him to be thrown out of his position in 1767. Wentworth distributed many territorial grants, always for a fee and keeping some of the land for himself. He established new townships extending to both sides of the Connecticut River and as far west as Bennington (named for Wentworth). These settlements, which included the eastern part of present day Vermont, came to be known as the "New Hampshire Grants."

New Hampshire also collided with the interests of New York for the land. Under the old grant of land by Charles II to the Duke of York, New York continued to claim "all the land from the west side of the Connecticut River to the east side of Delaware Bay." Before any decision could be

Joseph Blackburn: *Benning Wentworth.* 1760. New Hampshire Historical Society.

Benning Wentworth (1696-1770) was a leading merchant of Portsmouth. Appointed as governor of New Hampshire in 1741, he made vast grants of land not only in what was considered New Hampshire territory, but also on the west side of the river then claimed by New York. He included his friends, relatives, and himself among the beneficiaries. Forced to resign in 1767, he was succeeded by his nephew, John Wentworth who was one of the first trustees of Dartmouth.

Charlestown, New Hampshire, was known for many years as Township Number 4, the strongest outpost in the upper valley against the French and Indians. The fort, which had been the scene of a heroic defense by Phineas Stevens against the French and Indians in 1747, was used as an ammunition storage area and recruiting station during the Revolution. It eventually fell into disuse and disrepair, but now has been partially reconstructed. The stockade of Number 4 and eight other buildings have been completed, including the great hall with an attached four-story watch tower overlooking the Connecticut River. The fort presents a series of summer events including a military muster and a re-enactment of Stevens' battle.

made about the land, the colonists' attention was diverted by another war which began in 1745. Hostilities between the French and English were renewed in the War of the Austrian Succession, known in the colonies as King George's War.

To defend the northern boundaries, the colonists built a series of forts, the best known of which was "Number Four" at Charlestown. In 1747, a force of 700 French and Indians made a number of attacks along the northern boundaries and then laid siege to Fort Number Four. Captain Phineas Stevens and fifty men heroically defended the fort and refused to surrender, and the French and Indians ultimately withdrew.

Peace was officially declared in 1748, and the argument between New Hampshire and New York commenced again over the land between them. In 1751, it was agreed that the boundary issue should be "laid before His Majesty," but the intervention of another war — the last French and Indian war — prevented any determination of the matter by the Crown. This war between Britain and France was known in Europe as the Seven Years' War.

With the advent of hostilities, the upper valley again took on a strategic importance. Governor Wentworth sent Captain Peter Powers on an expedition to determine whether, as rumored, the French were fortifying the upper Connecticut. Powers went up the Merrimack River and across to the Connecticut at Piermont. He explored the river as far as Lancaster, but found no fort.

The war brought with it a renewal of the French and Indian raids. "Number Four," situated as it was in the line of march of the Colonial troops, bore the brunt of these attacks, and it became an important strategical point and headquarters for various Colonial regiments. It was at Charlestown in 1754 that a band of Indians broke into the Johnson home and seized seven people who, like the Deerfield victims of 1704, were marched to Canada and held captive for four years until they were eventually ransomed. Similar raids took place at Walpole below Bellows Falls and Hinsdale.

The importance of the upper valley as a route to the key fort of Crown Point on Lake Champlain, which had fallen to the French, made it imperative to build a road over the mountains to the fort. This was done in 1759 under orders from General Jeffrey Amherst who was in command of the British and colonial forces. The road began at Springfield, Vermont, passed west through Ludlow, and ended at Crown Point. It played a key role in events leading up to the collapse of French rule in Canada. When the road was completed, General Amherst recaptured Crown Point. Later, Major Robert Rogers and his Rangers made a punitive raid on the St. Francis Indians in which they killed the men and burned their women and children. The exhausted Rangers then worked their way back over the road to Round Island at the mouth of the Passumpsic River, where they were to meet up with a rescue party and supplies sent by General Amherst. However, the rescue party had come and gone, taking the supplies with them, because they feared Indian counterattacks. Rogers and three companions built a raft and floated down the river over the rapids to Fort Number Four. He came back with supplies and finally brought the survivors to the fort. Rogers became famous for his participation in this and subsequent campaigns, but he fought on the British side during the Revolution and died in obscurity in England.

By 1763, the war was over. French rule of Canada had ended, and with the elimination of the French threat, pressure for further upriver settlements was renewed with vigor. After an extensive survey of the river valley as far north as Fifteen Mile Falls, New Hampshire's Governor Wentworth issued new charters in 1761 for towns on both sides of the river up to Northumberland, some eighty miles north of Charlestown. Here again, he ran up against the New York claims to the land on the west of the river. The matter was again submitted to London, and, in 1764, New York emerged victorious when King George III declared "the western banks of the River Connecticut to be the boundary line between the said two provinces."

Although most boundary lines along American rivers extend to the center of the stream, New Hampshire has consistently claimed the entire bed of the Connecticut due to the wording of King George's 1764 decision. Its claim was upheld by the United States Supreme Court as late as 1933. Vermonters have really not been very unhappy about this assertion of rights since New Hampshire has been required to defray the complete cost of maintenance of the bridges.

After the King's ruling, which New Hampshire obviously disliked, the New York authorities tried to oust the settlers on the west bank or compel them to repurchase their lands. These moves were vigorously protested, both by the settlers and New Hampshire. Most of the settlers were young veterans from the French-Indian campaigns, and many had come from Connecticut. They had named their towns after Wethersfield, Windsor, Lebanon, Hartford, Lyme, — to name a few. They believed in local self-government which was quite different from the centralized authority prevailing in New York. Upper New York at the time was controlled in an almost feudal fashion by lords of the manor, such as the Rensselaers, the Livingstons, the Beekmans, and the Philipses.

Besides their differences with New York, the settlers also had very little in common with the Portsmouth ruling elite of New Hampshire. Therefore, they ignored the authorities from both New York and New Hampshire, and in 1770, organized themselves as the Green Mountain Boys under the leadership of Ethan Allen and his brother, Ira. Local townships were set up on an independent basis, no superior authority was admitted, and so the matter rested until the gradual emergence of the state of Vermont.

The lower river valley was little affected by the wars and problems of the upper valley. The French and Indians were no threat here, and there were no hindrances in the way of settling new towns. Prospering and improving their lifestyle were the important issues of the time for the colonists in Connecticut and lower Massachusetts.

Foremost among American theologians and metaphysicians in colonial days was Jonathan Edwards (1703-1758). Born in South Windsor, Connecticut, Edwards was pastor of the Northampton Church from 1727 to 1750. Following the strictest Calvinistic traditions of predestination, Edwards was a powerful preacher. He was the first of the great American revivalists, leading the "Great Awakening," as his crusade, which swept through the colonies, was called. His zeal was unbounded, but there was little cheer in his message when he would tell the world what a wicked place it was and what worse torments one could look forward to in the next. His most famous sermon was "Sinners in the Hand of an Angry God" in which he portrayed the fate of sinners, doomed to perdition, dangling over the searing flames of the fires of hell.

Edwards' views of hell and damnation were so unbending that he was dismissed by his congregation in 1750. Seven years later, he succeeded his son-in-law, Aaron Burr, as president of the College of New Jersey (now Princeton), but died a few months later. Edwards' grandson, Aaron Burr, was to play a significant role in American history some thirty or more years later.

Say-Brook Barr

LOTTERY,

To raise the Sum of *Five Hundred and Thirty Seven Pounds*, Lawful Money, to be laid out in fixing Buoys and other Marks, on and near the Mouth of Connecticut River, which will render the Navigation into and out of said River both safe and easy.

The SCHEME.

Number of Prizes.		Value of each		Dollars.
1 Prize	of	2000	is	2000
1 Do.	of	1000	is	1000
2 Do.	of	500	are	1000
12 Do.	of	100	are	1200
20 Do.	of	50	are	1000
50 Do.	of	20	are	1000
125 Do.	of	12	are	1500
700 Do.	of	8	are	5600
First Drawn		50	is	50
Last Drawn		50	is	50

911 Prizes
2689 Blanks

3600 Tickets, at 4 Dollars each, 14400
Subject to a Deduction of Twelve and a Half per Cent only, and not three Blanks to a Prize.

Said Lottery to begin Drawing on the 21st Day of September next—immediately after the drawing of which, a List of the fortunate Tickets will be advertised in the Hartford, New-Haven, New-London, Newport, Boston, and New-York News-Papers.

Tickets are to be sold by Mess. *Matthew Talcott, Richard Alsop* and *John Stocker* Middletown; *Ebenezer Plummer* of Glastenbury; *Silas Deane* of Wethersfield; *Samuel Olcott* and *John Chenevard* of Hartford, appointed by the General Assembly of this Colony, Managers of said Lottery, to be under Oath for the faithful Performance of their Trust.

N. B. Prizes not demanded within twelve Months after drawing, will be deemed as generously given by the Proprietors, to encourage the Design for which the above Lottery is granted, and be applied accordingly.

Hartford, June 5, 1773.

From the earliest days of the river settlements, the river remained unmarked, and the shoals were not dredged. In 1773, the Connecticut Assembly took action to mark the channels, shoals, and sandbars by authorizing a lottery to raise funds for that purpose.

Economically, the lower river valley was largely self-sufficient. Agriculture was the main occupation, but the farmers were, in one sense or another, versatile craftsmen able to take care of their own needs. Spinning, dying, and weaving were a few of the important household industries in the rural areas. Small gristmills were often developed in these areas to grind the grain. In the course of time, individuals became especially adept at a particular craft so that specialties began to develop in different trades, such as carpentry, masonry, blacksmithing, and shoemaking. These artisans became increasingly important in the towns.

Shipbuilding continued to grow, as maritime commerce increased and more ships were requested for Britain's royal navy. The largest shipyards were in Wethersfield, Middletown, Cromwell, East Middletown (as Portland was then known), the Haddams, Lyme, and Essex. Smaller shipyards were in Higganum, Chester, and Deep River.

Watercolor of Middletown in the late 18th century.

John Adams visited Middletown in 1771. The first part of the town he saw was known as the Upper Houses, now Cromwell. He recorded his impressions in his diary:

"Middletown, I think, is the most beautiful town of all. When I first came into the town, which was upon the top of a hill, there opened before me the most beautiful prospect of the river, and the intervals and the improvements on each side of it, and the mountains, at about ten miles distant, both on the east and west side of the river, and of the main body of the town at a distance. I went down this hill and into a great gate which led me right to the banks of the river and on the right hand is a fine level tract of interval land, as rich as the soils of Egypt . . . And after riding in this enchanting meadow for some time, you come to another gate which lets you into the body of the town, which is ornamented as is the meadow I just mentioned, with fine rows of trees and appears to me as populous, as compact, and as polite as Hartford. I wish the Connecticut flowed through Braintree."

The Hatheway House in Suffield, Connecticut, is considered one of New England's most important architectural landmarks of the eighteenth century. The main part of the house was built in 1760 and the north wing was added in 1795. The house, now owned by the Connecticut Antiquarian and Landmarks Society, reflects the prosperity of the merchant class at the time.

48

By the middle of the century, the larger towns in the river valley had achieved a good measure of prosperity. For instance, Middletown by 1756 was the most important port in Connecticut and the leading shipping center for the West Indies trade. With a population of 5,664, it was the largest and wealthiest town in the state. Out of fifty families residing on Main Street, seventeen were directly connected with the sea, either as shipbuilders, owners, carpenters, merchants, or ropemakers.

Wealthy merchants and shipbuilders in Middletown and other prospering towns built themselves substantial homes with well-planned interiors which reflected their prosperity. This, in turn, resulted in the growth of the decorative arts such as furniture, textiles, engravings, clocks, and silver. Cabinetmakers, pewterers, and silversmiths became important and respected craftsmen. In Middletown, Thomas Danforth was a leading pewterer. His business, which he began in the 1730s, grew and expanded over the next one hundred years. In addition to pewtermaking, he and the future Danforths manufactured a wide variety of hardware, and by 1818, Danforth branch stores or agencies had opened as far away as Philadelphia, Atlanta, and Savannah.

Cabinetmakers in the Connecticut River valley began to make the furniture which soon became classified under the names of valley communities: Windsor, Hartford, Glastonbury, Middletown, Hadley, and Hatfield. Many of their chests, tables, chairs, and other pieces eventually found their way into today's splendid collections of Old Deerfield, Sturbridge Village, and the Wadsworth Atheneum in Hartford, where they (can be seen today and) are being preserved for future generations.

Connecticut ships from the West Indies frequently brought back slaves who were used predominantly by wealthier citizens for household chores. By 1774, black slaves numbered about 6,500, or one-fortieth of the population of the river valley. A number of these were emancipated by their owners. The story of Venture Smith was the "Horatio Alger" story of the eighteenth century.

An extraordinary black African, Smith was born in Guinea in 1728 as a son of a king. Later sold into slavery, he was brought to Haddam by a sea captain. Smith eventually bought his freedom, and later acquired one hundred acres of land with three houses and twenty sailing vessels engaged in the river trade. His grave in the East Haddam cemetery is marked with a stone engraved:

> Sacred to the memory of Venture Smith, African, though the son of a king he was kidnapped and sold as a slave, but by his industry he acquired money to purchase his freedom, who died Sept. 19th, 1805 in ye 77th year of his age.

The increasing prosperity of the river valley brought with it a relaxation of some of the exacting Puritan strictures. Amusements, denounced earlier from the pulpits, were now made acceptable. Barn raisings, ship launchings, and corn huskings became occasions for partying and were accompanied by feasting and heavy drinking, particularly of cider and New England rum. Thanksgiving Day was a special day of celebration, but some years were to pass before Christmas was to become a day of merrymaking.

Education continued to be an important concern. When the century began, the colonists felt there should be institutions of higher learning in the valley. Their first endeavor to establish such an institution was to prove less than successful — at least in so far as the river valley was concerned.

In 1701, the Connecticut General Assembly desired to establish a college and granted a charter to "The Collegiate School." Saybrook was chosen as the site and Reverend Abraham Pierson, a distinguished and popular minister in Killingworth, was selected as the president. The Killingworth people, however, refused to let Pierson leave his ministry, so that the first classes were held in what is now Clinton. A few years later, after Pierson's death, the college was established in Saybrook, but some trustees and students preferred Hartford or New Haven. Meanwhile, the college received a library from Elihu Yale, an English philanthropist, and was renamed "Yale" in his honor. New Haven was finally successful in being designated as the site for the college, but when the trustees tried to remove the books from Saybrook, the citizens resisted with such force that the governor came to Saybrook and issued the following order:

> To Major John Clark of Saybrook
> Major of the County of New London
> Whereas I have been informed in Council that several Persons in your Town, have in a Riotous and tumultuous manner assembled, and have by threatenings declared themselves, with Resolutions to oppose with strong hand, by force and Arms & prevent the Execution of Orders, given by me in Council, pursuant to an Act of the Assembly holden in New Haven the 9th day of October last entituled and Act for the Encouragement of Yale Colledge, for the removal of the Books & papers, belonging to the sd. Colledge from Saybrook to the Library provided for them in the sd. Colledge in New Haven, whereby there is a great danger of the Peace being broken, by great & Notorious acts of Violence.
>
> You are hereby Commanded in his Majesties name, to cause your Drums to be beaten forthwith, and give order to all the officers and souldiers in the Train band, in your Town, to appear immediately in their Arms, who are hereby required to obey your Command and have them ready to attend you in the executing of such orders, as you shall receive from me, for the preventing all such riotous doing & mutinous proceedings. And hereof fail not, at your Peril. Given under my hand in Saybrook, this 4th day of December, In the fifth year of the Reign of Our Sovereign Lord George of Great Britain &c King Annoq. Dom. 1718.
>
> g. Saltonstall, Govr.

The books finally arrived in New Haven, but only after insults and rocks were exchanged and two highway bridges were destroyed. A good part of the books were found missing. And a tablet marking the site of Yale's beginnings can be found today not far from the site of the Saybrook Fort.

The second endeavor to establish an institution of higher learning was to prove more successful for the river valley, even if its original aim was never realized. In 1759, the Reverend Eleazar Wheelock established a school in Lebanon, Connecticut, for Christianized Indians, but meeting with local indifference and some hostility, he decided to move to another site. The offer of 3,000 acres of land, money, labor, and lumber prompted him to establish his college in Hanover, New Hampshire, in 1769, where peace finally had been made.

Wheelock named his college after the Earl of Dartmouth, who had been instrumental in raising financial support for it and in securing its

Joseph Stewart: *Eleazar Wheelock.* Dartmouth College. Eleazar Wheelock (1711-1779) was the first president of Dartmouth College. A poem by Richard Hovey, an early Dartmouth graduate, humorously described Wheelock's endeavor in moving his college from Connecticut to New Hampshire:

O, Eleazar Wheelock was a very pious man;
He went into the wilderness to teach the Indian,
With a Gradus ad Parnassum, a Bible and a drum
And five-hundred gallons of New England rum.

charter from George III. King George himself made a personal contribution to the college. Indian interest in the college was extremely limited from the beginning, and it was not long before Dartmouth became a college for white youth.

A legendary Dartmouth hero was John Ledyard, who entered the college in 1772. He left a year later in a canoe made with his own hands in which he went down the river to Hartford. He later sailed to Europe, Africa, and the West Indies, and joined up with Captain Cook on his voyage around the world. Ledyard died in Cairo in 1788 at the age of 37, on the threshold of an exploratory trip into the heart of Africa.

Connecticut people also cared about knowing the important events of the day. The first printing press had been established in 1709 in New London. Several newspapers later appeared, the most important being the *Connecticut Courant* which was established in 1764 in Hartford by Thomas Green. In 1770, Green turned the paper over to Ebenezer Watson, a young man of twenty-seven. Some years later Watson started a paper mill east of the river in order to have a readily available paper supply. The *Courant* is still carried on as the *Hartford Courant*, the oldest continuously published daily newspaper in the United States.

When Watson took over the paper, there were ferments in New England. Differences between the colonies and the mother country were becoming increasingly pronounced, and emotions were running strong. Watson, in his coverage of the news, took a staunch patriot line, and by the time of his premature death in 1777, the *Courant* had already established itself as one of the colonies' foremost patriot newspapers.

5

THE REVOLUTION AND ITS AFTERMATH

Affairs are hastening fast to a crisis, and the approaching campaign will in all probability determine forever the fate of America. Be exhorted to rise therefore to superior exertion on this great occasion; and let all that are able and necessary show themselves ready in behalf of their injured and oppressed country, and come forth to the help of the Lord against the mighty, and convince the unrelenting tyrant of Great Britain that they are resolved to be FREE.

Governor Jonathan Trumbull
June 18, 1776

The successful termination of the last French and Indian War was celebrated with great rejoicing in New England, coupled with professions of loyalty to Great Britain and the King. The enthusiasm, however, was short-lived.

Britain had previously undertaken strict regulation of Colonial trade, but had not enforced many of these measures. Now, at the behest of British mercantile and shipping interests, Parliament began to enforce these acts, thereby antagonizing merchants and commercial interests in the colonies. Next came the Stamp Act in 1765, designed to provide revenues for the defense and protection of the colonies and for the discharge of the enormous debts incurred by the prosecution of the French and Indian Wars. This act met with vigorous opposition in the colonies, particularly in Massachusetts and Connecticut. Mobs in Wethersfield and Hartford threatened Jared Ingersoll, the stamp tax collector. In Hartford, Governor Fitch, who had reluctantly supported the act, was ousted. After further mob violence, the Stamp Act was repealed.

The repeal of the Stamp Act was followed by other taxes and restrictions which brought about nonimportation agreements among the merchants. The British government then repealed these taxes and the situation quieted down, only to be aroused again by the tea monopoly granted to the East India Company. The Boston Tea Party of 1773 was followed by similar demonstrations in Connecticut. In Lyme, a peddler appeared with a hundred pounds of tea which the local matrons were boycotting. The men forthwith seized the intruder, confined him in the jail, and burned the tea in the middle of the street.

The British retaliated by closing the port of Boston to both overseas trade and coastal shipping, and handing down the Quebec Act which extended the boundaries of Quebec and reinstated the privileges of the Catholic Church. The staunchly Protestant colonists were outraged and referred to these measures as the Intolerable Acts. Strong support was voiced for Massachusetts. There followed the meeting of the First Continental Congress in September, 1774. Events moved rapidly, and the "shot heard round the world" was fired at Concord on April 19, 1775.

Within days, militiamen were marching from all parts of the valley to Cambridge under the leadership of Israel Putnam, Connecticut's rough and ready general. Legend has it that Putnam was plowing his farm in Pomfret, Connecticut, when he was told the news, and left so quickly for the war that he did not even unyoke his team.

The Connecticut Assembly met in special session to organize the Connecticut contribution to the war. It had become apparent that the American army in Massachusetts lacked the necessary cannons. On his way to Cambridge, Benedict Arnold, a native son of Norwich, Connecticut, pointed out that Fort Ticonderoga had a supply of cannons that probably could be seized.

A force was raised that included Ethan Allen and his Green Mountain Boys. In May, 1775, Arnold and Allen led the force up the river and across Lake Champlain. They seized Fort Ticonderoga "in the name of the great Jehovah and the Continental Congress." More cannons were seized at Crown Point. Over one hundred pieces were subsequently lugged over the hills and across the river to Boston. There, implanted on the hills of Dorchester overlooking the city, their presence alone compelled the British to evacuate in March, 1776, with little fighting.

Events took a swift course. Thomas Paine's pamphlet, "Common Sense," published in January, 1776, had made a profound impact. By March there were demands in the Continental Congress for independence, and this was finally realized in July with the signing of the Declaration. Among the Connecticut signatories was Oliver Wolcott of South Windsor, later to become governor of the state.

Now operations began in earnest. Several Connecticut regiments, sent to hold New York, participated in the Battle of Long Island and Washington's subsequent retreat. It was in the course of this campaign that Nathan Hale was executed as a spy.

A young graduate of Yale, Hale had taught school in East Haddam where his one-room schoolhouse still stands. Commissioned as an officer in the Connecticut militia, he volunteered to cross the enemy lines disguised as a schoolteacher to learn their plans, but he was discovered and hanged. Before undertaking his mission, Hale wrote a friend:

> I am fully sensible of the consequences of discovery and capture in such a situation. But for a year I have been attached to the army, and have not rendered any material service, while receiving a compensation, for which I make no return. Yet I am not influenced by the expectation of promotion or pecuniary reward; I wish to be useful, and every kind of service, necessary to the public good, becomes honourable by being necessary. If the exigencies of my country demand a peculiar service, its claims to perform that service are imperious.

The war seemed to drag on endlessly. The Continental Army morale was generally low. The New England states, like the others, did not fill their quota of soldiers, which had been established by Congress. Enlistments fell off, and desertions were widespread. To fill the quotas, many towns resorted to the offers of bounties. New Hampshire even enacted a draft law.

The Revolution was the first war since the time of the original settlements in which no military action took place in the river valley. In fact, after the evacuation of Boston, there was little action in all of New England other than the four raids on Danbury, Fairfield, New Haven, and New London, and the battle of Bennington in 1777. When Bourgoyne was advancing southward from Canada with the strategic objective of separating New England from the other colonies, he attempted to seize Bennington, an important supply place. A battle ensued in which he was thwarted by the Green Mountain Boys and General John Stark's New Hampshire militiamen.

There were threats against Saybrook, but nothing came of these other than a half-hearted attempt to establish a fort of sorts at the mouth of the river.

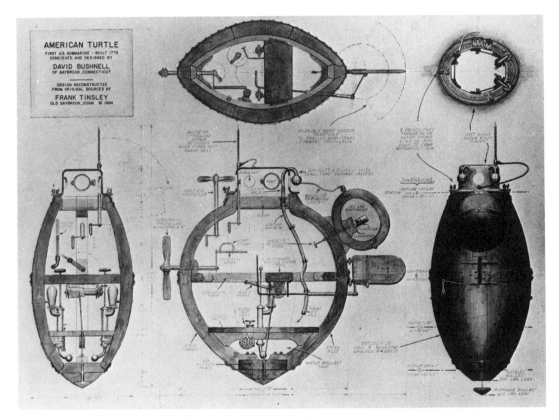

In 1775, David Bushnell of Westbrook invented the first submarine near what is now Otter Cove in Old Saybrook. Built of oak beams, it resembled the shells of two turtles joined together and was called the *American Turtle*. Bushnell won strong support for his invention, not only from Connecticut Governor Jonathan Trumbull and General Israel Putnam, but also from General George Washington and Benjamin Franklin. After successful trials on the river under the operation of Sergeant Ezra Lee of Lyme, the submarine was taken to New York. It made an unsuccessful attempt to destroy the *H.M.S. Eagle* of 64 guns, the flagship of the British fleet under Admiral Lord Howe. Two other attempts to sink British ships also ended in failure. Eventually, Bushnell left Connecticut and went to Georgia where he finished his years as a medical doctor under the name of Dr. David Bush. A replica of the submarine is on display at the Connecticut River Foundation's Museum in Essex.

One of the the most daring actions in the Revolution took place in May, 1777, when Colonel Return Jonathan Meigs of Middletown crossed Long Island Sound from Sachem's Head to Southold with 170 men in whaleboats. They had to carry their boats fifteen miles across a part of Long Island, they then crossed the Peconic Bay and attacked Sag Harbor where a British squadron was anchored. They burned twelve brigs and sloops filled with supplies and killed twelve and captured ninety of the enemy, all within twenty-four hours without losing one of their own men. They then returned to Connecticut, and Colonel Meigs was awarded the thanks of Congress and a suitably engraved sword.

Connecticut also contributed ships to the war. During the course of the war, thirteen ships saw service. Among these were the *Oliver*

Model of the *Oliver Cromwell,* built by John B. Comstock II, on display at the Connecticut River Foundation's Museum in Essex.

The *Oliver Cromwell* was built in 1776 at the Uriah Hayden Shipyard in Essex, one of the largest river shipyards at the time. This was a full-rigged vessel of 300 tons and carried twenty guns with a crew of 130 men. The ship was responsible for capturing nine British vessels before she surrendered under an attack by three British vessels in 1779. She was then refitted for service in the Royal Navy under the name, the *Restoration.*

Attributed to William Johnston: *Asbel Riley.* Connecticut Historical Society. Captain Asbel Riley of Wethersfield was commander of the brigantine, the *Ranger,* and preyed on British commerce in the West Indies in 1780. In the words of the British historian, George Trevelyan, the Americans "fastened eagerly upon an occupation which had an appearance of reconciling the claims of patriotic duty with the attractions of adventurous life, and the prospect of enormous gains."

Cromwell and the *Trumbull,* both built in river shipyards in 1776. The *Trumbull* was a thirty-six-gun frigate of 700 tons constructed in the Portland (then called Chatham) yards of John Cotton. Due to her size, it was not until 1779 that getting her over the Saybrook sandbar was accomplished, and then she was able to take part in several encounters with British ships.

More significant than the ships of war were the privateers that preyed on British merchantmen. Trade ships that were idled by the British blockade were commissioned as privateers with the state, owners, and crew splitting the proceeds of the prize. In the course of the war, several hundred privateers, many from the river towns of Hartford, Wethersfield, Middletown, East Haddam, Essex, and Saybrook, caused severe losses to British commercial interests.

One of the best known privateers was Captain Gideon Olmstead of East Haddam. He had sailed as a blockade runner to the West Indies where he had become the master of a French privateer. Later, captured by the British, he was being returned to New York when, along with three other Americans, he took over the ship and sailed into an American-held port. There he took command of the *Hawk,* owned by the Webbs of Wethersfield, and bought the *Raven* with a Hartford group. After having taken over a ship with sixteen guns and a crew of one hundred, he was recaptured by the British. His crew was imprisoned, and most of them died on the prison ships, but Olmstead was eventually exchanged and died in East Haddam in his ninety-seventh year.

Probably the most important contribution of the river valley to the Continental Army was in the form of provisions and supplies. Gun powder came from a number of Connecticut towns, including East Hartford and Glastonbury. Cannons, however, came from the iron works at Salisbury in western Connecticut. In 1778, Congress established a cannon factory at Springfield which was later to become the federal arsenal.

Lead for musket balls came from a rich lead mine on the banks of the river. As noted by Silas Deane in a letter from Middletown of May 23, 1775: "The state of the Lead Mine in this town has likewise engaged our attention. Upon enquiry, we find the ore is plenty and reputed rich, the vein is opened, seven tons of ore now raised and ready for smelting, and any other quantity may be had that may be required . . . . there can be no reasonable doubt, if we can succeed in refining, that this mine will abundantly supply, not only New England, but all the colonies with lead, in such plenty as to answer every demand of war or peace."

Connecticut merchants helped organize the supply of provisions for the army. A state commissary general was established in 1775 under the leadership of Joseph Trumbull, the son of Governor Trumbull. He was assisted by nine commissioners, including Colonel Henry Champion of Colchester and East Haddam, and Jeremiah Wadsworth of Hartford. Because of a state embargo that made the export of foodstuffs illegal without permit, the commissaries were able to purchase large quantities of foodstuffs, beer, rum, tobacco, soap, clothing, blankets, tools, lead, and bullets, and much more through private contracting in a noncompetitive market. These supplies were sent overland to the Continental Army.

The Continental Army Commissary was far from being so well organized and was constantly plagued with rivalries between state and congressional authorities, charges of corruption and graft, delays in payments to suppliers, and a constantly depreciating currency. Things improved for a while after Trumbull, at Washington's request, took over at the end of 1775, but continuing disputes with the Congress resulted in his resignation two years later.

The commissary became so disorganized that it was unable to supply meat to the Valley Forge Army in February, 1778, and the army was effectively saved only through a direct appeal from Washington to Governor Trumbull and the Connecticut Commissary. Henry Champion and Peter Colt scoured the river valley towns for live beef. Champion and his son, Epaphroditus, drove the first herd of 300 cattle overland from East Haddam to Valley Forge. (Some twenty years later, Epaphroditus became a prominent merchant in East Haddam. He had William Spratt design a handsome Federal house for him, which he called "The Terraces," with gardens sloping down to the riverbank. It was adjacent to the counting house and wharf where his ships unloaded their cargoes from the West Indies.)

Later, Jeremiah Wadsworth, at Washington's request, took over the Continental Army Commissary for a while, but continued bickerings prompted his resignation in 1779. The Congress then instituted a system of state requisitioning which resulted in even worse shortages in 1780 and 1781 when the states failed to meet their quotas. Throughout these last years, however, Connecticut continued to send supplies directly to Washington in response to his frequent appeals.

Dissatisfaction with the Continental Army commissary system led a number of Connecticut commissaries, including Jeremiah Wadsworth, to

John Trumbull: *Jeremiah Wadsworth and his son Daniel Wadsworth.* Wadsworth Atheneum. Jeremiah Wadsworth (1743-1804), a leading merchant of Hartford, played an outstanding role in the procurement of supplies for the Continental Army. Writing of Wadswoth in 1790, a French traveler, Jean Pierre Brissot, said: "Hartford is the residence of one of the most respectable men in the United States, Colonel Wadsworth. He enjoys a considerable fortune, which he owes entirely to his own labor and industry. Perfectly versed in agriculture and commerce, universally known for the service he rendered to the American and French armies during the war, generally esteemed and beloved for his great virtues, he crowns all his qualities by an amiable and singular modesty. His address is frank, his countenance open, and his discourse simple."

Newgate Prison in East Granby, Connecticut, was originally a copper mine dating from the beginning of the eighteenth century. It became a state prison in 1773 and was named for Newgate Prison in England. The prison was in use until 1827. During the Revolution, it was used to confine Tory sympathizers and prisoners of war who were considered especially dangerous. It is said that prisoners worked in the copper mines, while chained in iron collars, leg irons, and handcuffs. Grim tales remain of the lot of the prisoners of Newgate Prison.

become purchasing agents for the French forces of General Rochambeau who had arrived in Rhode Island in 1780. With the additional attraction of receiving payments in specie instead of Continental paper, suppliers from Eastern Connecticut developed a highly profitable trade in supplying the French forces.

During the war, Connecticut facilities were extensively used for the safekeeping of prisoners. The British captured at Ticonderoga were taken to Hartford. Prisoners who were considered dangerous were confined at Newgate Prison in East Granby. Others were quartered in various inland towns, including Middletown and Wethersfield, where they were more or less placed on parole on their word not to escape. William Franklin, the former royal governor of New Jersey, and an illegitimate son of Benjamin, was sent to Middletown where he became such a center of loyalist propaganda that he was removed to Litchfield and eventually ended up in England. Prisoner exchanges were frequent and were handled by Joseph Webb of Wethersfield.

The Joseph Webb House, built in 1752, was the site of the important meeting of Washington and Rochambeau in May, 1781. In addition to its historic importance, the house has considerable architectural distinction in its exterior and interior. The rooms, with their panelings, moldings, and fireplaces, portray the wealth and good taste that characterized Wethersfield in its colonial days. The house is part of the old settlement of Wethersfield, one of the best preserved historic districts in New England. Close to the house is the white, steepled Wethersfield Congregational Church, built in 1761, which was the first brick church in Connecticut. After a visit in 1774, John Adams recorded in his diary: "We went up to the steeple of the Meeting House from whence the most grand and beautiful prospect in the world." Adjacent to the church is the "burial place," the oldest stone of which dates from 1648.

River valley men took part in nearly all campaigns under Washington's command. Plans for the Battle of Yorktown were formulated by Washington and his French ally, Rochambeau, at the Joseph Webb House in Wethersfield in 1781. Governor Jonathan Trumbull, General Henry Knox, and Colonel Jeremiah Wadsworth were also at this meeting. As reported in the Hartford newspaper:

> On Saturday the 19th inst. his excellency General Washington, accompanied by Gen. Knox, Gen. Du Portail, and their respective suites, arrived at Wethersfield; as he dismounted at his quarters he was saluted by the discharge of thirteen cannon, the corps of Artillery, under the command of Capt. Frederick Bull. On Monday, the 21st instant, his excellency the Count du Rochambeau, commanding the army of his most Christian Majesty at Newport, Gen. Chatteleu, and their suites, arrived at Wethersfield. They were met at Hartford, by his excellency General Washington, the officers of the army, and a number of gentlemen, who accompanied them to Wethersfield, where they were saluted with the discharge of cannon. Every mark of attention and politeness were shewn their excellencies, and the other gentlemen of the allied armies whilst attending the convention.

Silas Deane, a wealthy lawyer and merchant, was another prominent Wethersfield man of the time. A Connecticut delegate to the Continental Congress, he was sent to France in 1776 as America's first diplomat. He not only secured the shipment of arms and munitions for the struggling colonies, but also enlisted the services of LaFayette, DeKalb, Von Steuben, and Pulaski. Deane signed the Treaty of Alliance with France. However, he made his share of enemies and was falsely accused of embezzlement of government funds, only to be exonerated long after his death in 1789. Deane is still remembered in Wethersfield by his house, which is next door to Webb's house and open to the public, and by a commercial highway which bears his name.

Leading Connecticut throughout the Revolution was Governor Jonathan Trumbull, who had been popularly elected in 1774. He was the only Colonial governor to have supported independence and to have been retained in office throughout the war. In Massachusetts, General Gage took over from the last royal governor of the state in 1774. One year later, however, Gage evacuated Boston with his troops, leaving Massachusetts, in effect, independent with a provisional congress in control. In New Hampshire, the once popular governor, John Wentworth, fled from Portsmouth on June 13, 1775 under threat from a mob. On January 5, 1776, New Hampshire was the first of the colonies to establish a government wholly independent of Great Britain.

The surrender of Cornwallis at Yorktown in October, 1781, ended the fighting, but the British continued to hold the principal seaports of New York, Philadelphia, Baltimore, Charleston, an Savannah. The war, however, had become quite unpopular in England where there was considerable sympathy for the colonists, and there was little support for any further campaigns. A peace treaty was finally signed in Paris in 1783. Britain recognized the independence of the colonies, established their boundaries, and agreed to withdraw from the ports it still occupied. However, the British West Indies markets remained closed to American trade.

Economic restrictions were soon relaxed, and shipping and commerce were renewed to the Dutch, French, and Danish West Indies. The

John Trumbull: *Jonathan Trumbull* (taken from a larger portrait, 1774) Connecticut Historical Society. Jonathan Trumbull (1710-1785), governor of Connecticut from 1769 to 1784, rendered great services to Washington and the Continental Army. His administration of Connecticut from colony to independence and statehood brought great stability to the state. As noted in the 1810 Gazetteer:

> "The revolution, which so essentially affected the government of most of the colonies, produced no very perceptible alteration in the government of Connecticut. While under the jurisdiction of Great Britain, they elected their own governors, and all subordinate civil officers, and made their own laws, in the same manner, and with as little control as they now do. Connecticut has ever been a republic; and perhaps as perfect and as happy a republic as ever existed. While other states more monarchical in their government and manners, have been under a necessity of undertaking the difficult talk of altering their old, or forming new constitutions, and of changing their monarchical for republican manners, Connecticut has uninterruptedly proceeded in her old track, both as to government and manners; and, by these means, has avoided those convulsions which have rent other states into violent parties."

basic occupation of the valley, however, was still agriculture, and farming was in a state of depression because of the inflationary currency, large debts, and the loss of the British West Indies markets. Emigration increased northward to Vermont and New Hampshire, and westward to the "Western Reserve" in what is now the area around Cleveland, Ohio. In 1786, Connecticut had received this land, and for some thirty years Connecticut families emigrated there in search of cheap land and low taxes.

In western Massachusetts, the farmers' discontent culminated in a rebellion in 1787. Led by Daniel Shays, a former officer of the Continental Army, embittered farmers attacked the federal arsenal at Springfield, but they were defeated. Eventually reforms were enacted, Shays and his associates received federal pardons, and peace and prosperity returned to the area.

During these years, the colonies formed a loose association under the Articles of Confederation. These were found to be wholly ineffective to meet the political and economic problems of the republic. Connecticut sent a distinguished delegation to the Constitutional Convention of 1787 in Philadelphia. Oliver Ellsworth of Windsor, later senator and chief justice of the United States, was one of the delegates. When the success of the

Ralph Earl: *Oliver and Abigail Ellsworth.* Wadsworth Atheneum.

Oliver Ellsworth was a Princeton graduate of 1766, although most prominent men in Connecticut at the time went to Yale. Ellsworth had entered Yale first, only to find that his exuberant personality clashed with Yale rigidity, so he transferred to Princeton. Ellsworth was a member of the Continental Congress, author of the so-called Connecticut Compromise in the Constitutional Convention of 1787, U.S. senator, third chief justice of the United States, and minister to France's Napoleon.

Ellsworth lived at Elmwood in Windsor, shown in the painting. When the house was originally built in 1740, it was quite simple, and Ellsworth made many additions and improvements. Washington, LaFayette, and President John Adams were among the visitors at Elmwood. Ellsworth was well travelled, but his heart was in Connecticut. Shortly before his death, he wrote: "I have visited several countries, and I like my own the best. I have been in all States of the Union, and Connecticut is the best State. Windsor is the pleasantest place in Connecticut. I am content, perfectly content, to die on the banks of the Connecticut." And, indeed, Ellsworth did die at Elmwood on November 26, 1807.

Prominent among Hartford landmarks today is the fine Old State House, designed by Charles Bulfinch (1763-1844), and built between 1793 and 1796. It took the place of an earlier wooden structure which had served some sixty years, albeit inadequately. That building had been severely damaged in an accidental fire during the fireworks celebration on the occasion of the news of the peace treaty with Great Britain. It was in this earlier state house that Abraham Davenport immortalized himself on May 19, 1780, during a session of the General Assembly. There was an eclipse of the sun, and the sky became so dark that the members feared Judgment Day was about to come. Said Davenport to his colleagues, "I am against adjournment. The Day of Judgment is either approaching or it is not. If it is not, there is no cause for adjournment; if it is, I choose to be found doing my duty. I move therefore that candles be brought."

It was in the Bulfinch State House that the Hartford conventions of 1815 and 1818 were held, and LaFayette and Marshall Foch were made honorary citizens of Hartford. The building served on an alternating basis with New Haven as Connecticut's capitol from 1796 to 1879. Then it was seriously threatened by demolition, but has now been fully restored to its original beauty.

convention was imperiled by the rivalry of the larger and smaller states, Connecticut came up with the compromise under which each state was given equal representation in the senate and proportional representation in the house based on population. After vigorous popular debates, Connecticut, by a vote of 128 to forty, became the fifth state to ratify the Constitution. Massachusetts and New Hampshire followed shortly thereafter.

The years following 1790 saw a prosperous and contented society in New England and the Connecticut River Valley. Liberty and self-rule had been achieved. The Constitution gave the former colonies a sense of national unity and stability. The post-war depression had given way to a broad prosperity. Agriculture, commerce, and shipbuilding revived.

Transportation improved between the towns and on the river. Bridges were built across the river, replacing some of the ferries. The first bridge across the river had been built in 1784 at Bellows Falls. It was 365 feet long and fifty feet above the river. It was heralded as being "equal to any bridge ever built in America . . ." for elegance, strength, and public utility. The next covered bridge was built in 1796 between Windsor and Cornish.

(It is popularly believed that bridges were covered in order to prevent the accumulation of snow during the winter, but the situation is, in fact, quite the reverse. The purpose of the covering was to preserve the timbers from rotting away and, indeed, in the past, snow was actually brought onto the bridge in order to permit sleighs to make the crossing.)

Ralph Earl: *Colonel Samuel Talcott*. Wadsworth Atheneum.

Earl's portrait of Talcott represents a prosperous gentleman of taste and means in the 1790s. Talcott had commanded a regiment in the expedition against Crown Point and was a leading citizen of Hartford before and after the revolution. As was sometimes the custom of the time, the artist used the window in the painting to show Talcott's property with the church spires of Hartford in the distance. Hartford in 1790 was described by Jean Pierre Brissot:

"To describe the neighborhood of Hartford is to describe Connecticut. Nature and art have here displayed all their treasures; it is really the paradise of the United States. The state owes all its advantages to its situation. It is a fertile plain, enclosed between two mountains which render difficult its communications by land with the other states. It is watered by the superb Connecticut River, safe and easy to navigate, which flows into the sea. The riches of this state are here more equally divided, since they are based upon agriculture. There is here more equality, less misery, more simplicity, more virtue, more of everything which constitutes republicanism."

Typical of the architectural simplicity in the rural areas of the river valley is the Old Meeting House in Chester, Connecticut. Built in 1793, it has been in continuous use since that time, originally as a meeting house and church and subsequently as a town hall, theater, and community center. The front portico was added to the building in 1876 when the interior was rebuilt into a theater with a Victorian, horseshoe-shaped gallery.

Another meeting house of the time is in Rockingham, Vermont. Austere and stark in architecture, with a high pulpit and boxed pews, this 1787 building is still in use as a church.

A canal, the first on the river and also probably the first in the United States, was opened in 1795 to circumvent the falls at South Hadley. Shortly thereafter, two more canals were opened, one at Bellows Falls and the other in Turners Falls, Massachusetts.

The river itself was still very shallow in parts with an average depth of less than six feet, but at the instigation of Jeremiah Wadsworth, a company was organized to dredge the riverbed and to make other improvements. By 1795, commerce on the river had so increased that a new United States Custom House was built in Middletown, which was still the largest port in Connecticut.

Along with the growth of prosperity came the time to promote education, and enjoy literature and drama. The Deerfield Academy was established in 1797, and its Memorial Hall, now a colonial museum, was built in 1798. The first literary circle in America, the Hartford Wits, became famous. Originally interested in the modernization of the Yale curriculum, this group of Yale graduates soon became known as a conservative Federalist enclave, venting their satires on the Jeffersonian Republicans. Included in the group were Timothy and Theodore Dwight, Joel Barlow, John Trumbull (a cousin of the painter), Lemuel Hopkins, Robert Alsop, and General David Humphreys.

Joel Barlow was one of the best known of the Hartford Wits. In 1787, he wrote an epic poem, *The Vision of Columbus*, which opened with the following lines:

> I sing the mariner who first unfurled
> An eastern banner o'er the western world,
> And taught mankind where future empires lay
> In these fair confines of descending day.

The Connecticut River was one of Columbus' visions:

> Thy stream, my Hartford, through its misty robe,
> Played in the sunbeams, belted far the globe.
> No watery glades through richer vallies shine,
> Nor drinks the sea a lovelier wave than thine.

Barlow later broke with his Federalist friends. While in Paris during the French Revolution, he actively supported the Republicans. In Algiers as U.S. Consul in 1795, he was able to secure the release of prisoners held for ransom, and he negotiated treaties with the so-called Barbary states. Sent to Europe to negotiate a treaty with Napoleon, he died in 1812 from exposure suffered during Napoleon's retreat from Moscow.

In Vermont, Royall Tyler of Guilford, a Revolutionary War soldier, wrote the first comedy in the American theater, "The Contrast." Later, he and Joseph Dennie published a weekly newspaper, "The Farmer's Museum," which had a wide circulation along the entire eastern seaboard. President Washington was one of its readers. In 1797, Tyler wrote *The Algerine,* the first American novel to be republished in England. Tyler later became chief justice of the Vermont supreme court.

Vermont's status as a state remained unsettled throughout the Revolution and a number of subsequent years. There was constant feuding with the New York provincial authorities. On March 13, 1775, Westminster had been the scene of armed resistance to New York in what Vermonters call the Westminster Massacre. New York officials had attempted to forcibly suppress an attempt by a local group to prevent a court session, and two Vermonters had been killed.

Later that year, the river towns brought a petition to the King "to be taken out of so offensive a jurisdiction and either annexed to some other government or re-erected and incorporated into a new one."

After Lexington and Concord "rendered any petition to the King inexpedient," the Continental Congress of 1776 was requested to recognize Vermont as a separate juridical entity, but no action was taken. The next year, a meeting was held at Westminster at which the entire west side of the river was declared an independent state under the name of "New Connecticut." At a later convention in Windsor, the name Vermont was adopted because the name "New Connecticut" was already used as a name for the Western Reserve.

In the meantime, towns on the New Hampshire side of the river, most of which had been settled by Connecticut farmers who had little in common with the Portsmouth gentry, wanted to establish a new state in the river valley. They visualized the state would embrace the western half of New Hampshire and the eastern side of Vermont, and would have its center at Hanover. In 1778, sixteen New Hampshire towns joined with the Vermont river towns in this effort under the leadership of Dartmouth President Eleazar Wheelock.

The "College Party," as it was called, was not unwilling to let New York have the Vermont land west of the Green Mountains, but not so Ethan Allen who, after being captured by the British in 1775 in an ill-fated expedition against Montreal, had returned to Vermont in a prisoner exchange. He and his brothers owned some 300,000 acres in central Vermont which they did not wish to give up, and they vigorously resisted the efforts of the "College Party." Eventually, under pressure from New Hampshire and, more importantly, from the Continental Congress in Philadelphia where they were seeking admission as the fourteenth state, Vermont officials rejected the sixteen New Hampshire towns.

Thus appeased, New Hampshire was willing to acquiesce in any decision of the Continental Congress on the status of Vermont, but New York continued to refuse to recognize the Vermont claims. In 1779, a New York militia company was sent into Vermont to protect New York sympathizers from Ethan Allen and his Green Mountain Boys. Allen's Boys proceeded to arrest the New York militia officers.

It was at Windsor, in July, 1777, that Vermont's first constitutional convention was held at which Vermont's independence was reaffirmed, and the name of the new state was changed from New Connecticut to Vermont. At the same time a constitution was adopted which, among other things, abolished slavery (being the first to do so) and established universal manhood suffrage without property or income qualifications. The Old Constitution House, formerly a tavern, still stands and is now a museum of early Vermont memorabilia.

The Old South Church in Windsor, Vermont, built in 1798, is considered to be one of the masterpieces of the American architect, Asher Benjamin (1773-1845). Benjamin was originally from Greenfield, Massachusetts, where his works included the Public Library, the Brick House, and the Coleman-Hollister House. He is best known for his drawings and manuals of the architecture of the late Colonial and Greek Revival periods which were used by local carpenters. In all, he wrote seven books which went through forty-four editions so that, in effect, his books were among the first in the "do-it-yourself" category.

Another squabble between New York and Vermont took place in Guilford. In 1772, its inhabitants had voted to join New York, and the Vermont partisans refused to acquiesce. So, for a number of years, there were two sets of town officials, two town meetings, and varying degrees of violence on both sides. Finally Ethan Allen arrived in 1783 with his Green Mountain Boys and issued his proclamation: "I, Ethan Allen, declare that unless the people of Guilford peaceably submit to the authority of Vermont, the town shall be made as desolate as were the cities of Sodom and Gomorrah, by God." Although Allen then declared martial law and collected the back taxes claimed by Vermont, the anarchy continued.

The Allen brothers even engaged in intrigues with the British authorities in Canada, looking to the possible union of Vermont with the loyalist Canadian provinces.

Eventually, New York relinquished her claims for $30,000, and Vermont was admitted to the Union in 1791 as the fourteenth state, but Allen did not live to see the day, having died two years previously.

Ethan Allen, the folk hero of Vermont, was ever the controversial character. An eighteenth century deist in orthodox New England, he made many enemies in the conservative communities of the river valley. Four years before his death, he published *Reason, the Only Oracle of Man*, attacking Christianity in general and New England Calvinism in particular. The book was roundly condemned by the leading divines of the day. On Allen's death, Yale president Ezra Stiles wrote with pious certainty: "Feb. 12 — Genl. Ethan Allen of Vermont died & went to hell this day." And yet, whatever his faults, Allen was not bereft of prayers for the salvation of his soul, for his daughter Fanny was to become the first Catholic nun in New England.

6

THE EARLY NINETEENTH CENTURY VALLEY

The New Englanders were very well satisfied with themselves in 1790 and had reason to be; they had struck root in a region where nature was not lavish, produced a homogeneous and happy society, won liberty, and, by their own enterprise, got out of the depression. Disorderly when royal governors attempted to thwart their will, the Yankees had sloughed off cruder phases of democracy; for another generation the leadership of their clergy, well-to-do merchants, and conservative lawyers would not be successfully challenged.

Samuel Eliot Morison
The Growth of the American Republic

At the turn of the nineteenth century, the Connecticut River valley from the Canadian border to the mouth of the sound presented a cohesive geographical area, with the river itself serving as the principal avenue of communication. Communities in the upper valley maintained their principal links with Springfield and Hartford via the river. Overland journeys to Boston were difficult and hazardous, and it was not until the age of the railroad, in the middle of the century, that the communities in the upper valley solidified their connections with coastal Massachusetts and New Hampshire.

The 1810 census showed a total population of all of the towns of Connecticut, Massachusetts, New Hampshire, and Vermont, bordering on the

RIVER TOWN POPULATIONS IN 1810

Connecticut		Massachusetts	
Saybrook	3,996	Springfield	2,767
Lyme	4,321	West Springfield	3,109
Haddam	2,205	Northampton	2,631
East Haddam	2,537		
Middletown	5,372	**Vermont**	
Portland	3,258	Springfield	2,115
Wethersfield	3,961	Windsor	2,757
Hartford	6,003		
East Hartford	3,240	**New Hampshire**	
East Windsor	3,081	Claremont	2,094
Windsor	2,868	Hanover	2,135

Samuel F.B. Morse: *The Family of Jedidiah Morse of Charlestown, Massachusetts.* 1811. Smithsonian Institution.

Jedidiah Morse (1760-1826), a Congregational clergyman, was known as the "father of American geography." He produced a series of books including The *American Gazetteer* which first appeared in 1797 with subsequent editions in 1804 and 1810. It provides excellent references to conditions at the time. His son, Samuel, was not only one of the leading American painters of his day, but also the principal developer of the electric telegraph and the author of the Morse Code.

Connecticut River, as 129,000. Of these, 48,000 were in Connecticut, 17,000 in Massachusetts, 25,000 in New Hampshire, and, surprisingly, 39,000 were in Vermont. (Vermont's total population fifty years earlier had been less than 1,000.)

The population of the river valley was fairly homogeneous, being principally of English extraction. The *American Gazetteer* of 1810 described the people of Connecticut as a "wise and virtuous people, well informed and jealous of their rights; and whose external circumstances approach nearer to equality than those, perhaps, of any other people in a state of civilization, in the world . . . the bulk of the inhabitants are industrious, sagacious husbandmen." (Jedidiah Morse, the editor of the *Gazetteer*, might be accused of lack of objectivity because he was born in Woodstock, Connecticut.)

The people living in western Massachusetts and along the river in Vermont and New Hampshire were of similar stock. Hampshire County in Massachusetts, which then included the entire river valley in that state, was described as "one of the most fertile and populous counties in the United States." Vermont people were an "industrious, brave, hardy, active, and frugal race."

As to New Hampshire, the *Gazetteer* noted that "on the Connecticut River, the inhabitants emigrated chiefly from Connecticut, and, in some degree, exhibit the literary and religious character of that state." The *Gazetteer* took a more jaundiced view of the eastern part of the state, noting, by way of contrast, that "it was settled by people whose object was commerce" and that "their descendents have, in a great degree, inherited their character and show that disregard for science and religion, generally connected with that employment. Ardent spirits are drunk and a roughness of manners indulged." The same observation could well be made on the differences between the river Vermonters, who were as staid and conservative as their Connecticut forebears, and the western Vermonters, typified by the Allens and their friends who were mainly interested in cheap land and also indulged in "ardent spirits" and "a roughness of manners."

Politically, everything seemed serene and orderly in conservative New England. The leadership was in the hands of the commercial and shipping interests, the successful merchants, the clergy, and the lawyers. Most of them were staunch Federalists who looked askance at Jeffersonian Republicanism, equating it with atheism, egalitarianism and terror, all too well exemplified by the French Revolution. Property rights were respected, and the vote was restricted to those with property qualifications, except in Vermont.

Of all the New England states, Connecticut at this time appeared to be the most conservative. The *Gazetteer* describes the Connecticut political climate:

> To vote for legislators a person must take the freeman's oath. No person is allowed to take this oath till he is approved by the selectmen of the town, and two justices of the peace, as a man of peaceable behavior, and good moral character, and also that he possesses a freehold estate of £40. Hence there is never such a low mob at elections here as in some neighboring states. He who has the most merit, not he who has the most money, is generally chosen into publick office. As instances of this it is to be observed, that many of the citizens of Connecticut, from the humble walks of life, have risen to the first offices in the state, and filled them with dignity and reputation. That base business of electioneering, which is so directly calculated to introduce wicked and designing men into office, is yet but little known in Connecticut. A man who wishes to be chosen into office, acts wisely for that end, when he keep his desires to himself. A thirst for learning prevails among all ranks of people in this state. More of the young men in Connecticut, in proportion to their numbers, receive a publick education, than in any of the states . . . . That party spirit, however, which is the bane of political happiness, has not raged with such violence in this state as in Massachusetts and Rhode Island. Public proceedings have been conducted generally with much calmness and candor. The people are well informed as to their rights, and judicious in securing them. Political tranquility and unanimity follow. All religions, that are consistent with the peace of society, are tolerated in Connecticut.

These years brought with them a vast expansion of foreign commerce. The renewal of the wars in Europe between France and other European powers led by Great Britain, benefited neutral America whose shipping was now to be seen on the seven seas. Much of this shipping originated from the river valley where trade along the Atlantic seaboard and with the

Wheelock House in 1869, built 1817-1821, second from southern end of the Ridge, Orford, N.H.

Orford, New Hampshire is a delightful, small town and a rural center of culture and some wealth today. There is a beautiful row of seven Greek Revival houses, built between 1773 and 1839. They are surrounded by spacious lawns and white picket fences, and are known as the Ridge Houses. Sometimes this is called Bulfinch Row because one of the houses was said to have been designed by Charles Bulfinch. The row is on the easterly side of Orford's single straight street bordered by maples and elms. It bespeaks eloquently of the elegance and comfort of the builders of the houses. The General John Wheeler House, built in 1814, and the southernmost on the row, is believed to have been designed by Asher Benjamin, then an associate of Bulfinch in Boston. The third house from the south was owned by Samuel Morey of steamboat fame. Washington Irving visited Orford and wrote, "In all my travels in this country and Europe, I have never seen any village more beautiful than this. It is a charming place; nature has done her utmost here."

Thomas Low Nichols, pioneer dietician and hydrotherapist, was born in Orford in 1815. He has described Orford and the Coos Country as it was in the middle of the nineteenth century:

"My native State glows in my memory, — a land of craggy mountains, whose summits glisten in the sun, or fade in the blue distance; of silvery lakes cradled in the forests and among the hills; of crystal springs, singing brooks, roaring waterfalls, and clear arrowy rivers, swollen in the springtime to magnificent torrents; of the loveliest of green valleys, walled by the grandest of precipitous mountain ranges, with villages of white cottages and mansions with green blinds, shaded by broad-spreading elms and shining sugar-maples. The forests are pine, hemlock, spruce, odorous balsam-fir, the great white birch (of whose bark the Indians made canoes, and which I rolled into torches for night fishing), beech, maple, oak, and more trees than I can remember. The ground was fragrant with pine-leaves, mosses, and the wintergreen, with its bright red berries, alive with playful squirrels and musical with singing birds. A glowing landscape in summer; in winter a robe of glittering snow.

"The broad intervals on the rivers are fertile. The hills are excellent pasturage, where the stones allow grass to grow between them. Orchards of apples, pears, cherries, and plums also flourish with great vigor; so would hardy grapes, for there are wild ones in abundance along the borders of every stream. In my boyhood the population of this State was about 250,000, mostly agricultural. All the best lands were occupied, and a surplus population was already emigrating to the richer country of Western New York and Ohio. A farmer-proprietor, having from one hundred to three hundred acres of land, 'suitably divided into arable, pasturage and woodland,' might have half a dozen sons and as many daughters. Such a farm does not divide to advantage. One son, not always the eldest, takes the homestead, assuming the support of his parents in their old age, and any unmarried aunts or sisters; the rest go out to make their way in the world. One becomes a lawyer, another a doctor, another a merchant, an editor, a politician, member of Congress, cabinet minister, president perhaps; who knows? Daniel Webster was the son of a New Hampshire farmer; so was General Cass, and Horace Greeley, and Long John Wentworth. In a group of distinguished men of various professions in a western town I have recognized four or five as sons of New Hampshire farmers, who, as boys, had held the plow, and hardened their bodies with useful toil, while they picked up their education at the common school, or by the light of pine-knots blazing in the kitchen fireplace.

"Orford, in which I was born, had about 1,000 inhabitants. There was a pretty village with a Congregational meeting-house, post office, tavern, two or three stores, each with its assortment of draperies, ironmongery, groceries, wines, liquors, tobacco, crockery, glass — almost everything, in fact. There were also two or three lawyers, and a blacksmith, hatter, shoemaker, wheelwright, cabinet-maker, tailor. Grist-mills which ground our corn, and saw-mills which supplied our timber, were upon a mill brook which brawled down from the hills and wound through the loveliest of meadows into the Connecticut. There were no landlords. Almost every man owned the land he cultivated. The proprietor of hundreds of acres worked harder than any man he could hire. And whom could he hire? There were very few men to go out at 'day's works'. The two or three richest men in our parts were wildly reputed to be worth forty or fifty thousand dollars. The farmer who made both ends meet, with a little increase of his stock, thought himself doing well enough."

Nichols also recounted Orford's July 4th celebration with "the shining river winding off into the distance, the village with white houses embowered in trees, the sky intensely blue, and the glorious July sunshine. The music was a fife and drum. The militia company of our district was posted on the field, and later in the day fired off a rattling *feu-de-joie*. There was a salute, to open the ceremonies." Then came a prayer, "followed by the inevitable reading of the Declaration of Independence, the oration, another salute from the old flintlock muskets, and then an attack upon the bread and cheese and rum-punch provided by the committee."

Dutch, Danish, and French West Indies was an important factor in the economy. As described in Morse's *Gazetteer:*

> The trade of Connecticut is principally with the West-India islands, and is carried on in vessels from 60 to 140 tons. The exports consist of horses, mules, oxen, oak staves, hoops, pine boards, oak planks, beans, Indian corn, fish, beef, pork, &c. Horses, like cattle, and lumber, are permitted in the Dutch, Danish, and French ports. A large number of coasting vessels are employed in carrying the produce of the state to other states. To Rhode-Island, Massachusetts and New-Hampshire, they carry pork, wheat, corn and rye. To North and South-Carolina, and Georgia, butter, cheese, salted beef, cider, potatoes, hay, &c. and receive in return, rice, indigo and money. But as New-York is nearer, and the state of the markets always well known, much of the produce of Connecticut, especially of the western parts, is carried there; particularly pot and pearl ashes, flax feed, beef, pork, cheese, and butter in large quantities. Most of the produce of Connecticut river from the adjacent parts of Massachusetts, New-Hampshire and Vermont, as well as of Connecticut, goes to the same market.

Most of the products for the foreign trade came from the land and, for the first years of the century, agriculture and cattle raising retained their importance in the river economy.

Orchard plantings were developed, and as stated by an editor of the time, "there is probably no part of the United States in which the growth of apples is so sure as upon the Connecticut River." Cider was distilled into a brandy. Gin was also an important staple and a valuable export and was said to be of "excellent quality." There were twenty-one gin distilleries around the Windsors and Warehouse Point. In 1810, there were 125 distilleries in Vermont, but none were left by 1850.

Tobacco continued to be an important crop in the area from Hartford to Deerfield. Cigarmaking originated in 1810 in Suffield. Simeon Viets brought in a Cuban to teach the local women to roll the tobacco leaf as a wrapper, and the so-called Spanish cigar was born.

The Noah Webster House in West Hartford is an eighteenth century farmhouse, erected like many of its contemporaries around a massive center chimney. Here was born Noah Webster in 1758, one of the five children of a farmer. Noah left the farm to attend Yale, but returned to live there while he taught school in the Hartford area. Webster's school teaching led him to write his Speller and Grammar, among the first schoolbooks in America. He later compiled a 70,000 word dictionary which was published in Springfield, Massachusetts, in 1828. Webster was a man of many parts: teacher, lecturer, writer, as well as lawyer, editor and legislator. Later residing in Springfield, he was one of the founders of Amherst College.

COMSTOCK, FERRE & CO'S PRICES OF TURNIP SEEDS.

Seed Farm and Gardens,
WETHERSFIELD, CONN., Aug. 1, 1860.

Sir:

Having secured our crops of Turnip Seed in fine order, we have on hand a large supply of the leading kinds of our own growth, all from transplanted roots of the very best stocks. We now offer them at greatly reduced prices, much lower than we have sold them before.

English Cabbage, Ruta Baga and other English Turnip Seeds, are much higher this year, in consequence of the loss of roots by the severe weather of the last winter in England.

Prices without any Discount.

Early Flat Dutch Spring Turnip,	. . .	30 cts. per lb.	$25 per 100 lbs.
Strap-leaf Red Top Flat, "	. . .	30 " "	25 " "
" " White Flat, "	. . .	30 " "	25 " "
Long White Cow-horn, "	. . .	40 " "	35 " "
Sweet Yellow Globe, "	. . .	45 " "	40 " "
Large English Norfolk, "	. . .	40 " "	35 " "
Large White Globe, "	. . .	40 " "	35 " "
C. F. & Co's. Premium Flat Dutch Cabbage, the very best in America,	.	1.75 " "	150 " "

Seeds in Papers.

Under 1000 papers,	. . . . .	2.50 per 100 papers.
Over 1000 "	. . . . . .	2.25 " "
Over 3000 "	. . . . .	2.00 " "

When 4000 papers are ordered, the card of the purchaser will be printed on every paper without charge, if the order is given in time.

Having the prospect of very abundant crops, with exception of Onion, we are in expectation of being able to reduce the price of several other seeds, and will send you our General Price List, when published. In the mean time you may send us your early orders, relying upon our not being undersold by any respectable house in the trade.

During the last three or four years, Messrs. Comstock and Ferre have in great measure withdrawn their personal attention from the business of C. F. & Co., and left the management of its details to an employee, who has for good reasons been discharged, and they now again give their personal supervision to every department. Customers may rely as formerly upon their orders being filled with accuracy and dispatch.

Yours Respectfully,

COMSTOCK, FERRE & CO.

Comstock, Ferre, & Company in Wethersfield was established in 1820. It is still in the same location and is the oldest seed company in continuous operation in the United States.

The other special crop of the river valley was the onion. It was said that more onions were grown around Wethersfield than in any other place on the continent. Indeed, in 1819, The Pease and Niles *Gazetteer* noted that Wethersfield was "the only town in the state which makes a business of the cultivation of this excellent root. It is particularly novel and interesting on passing through the town in the month of June to behold in every direction the extensive fields of onions. Whilst in a luxurious state for vegetation, the growing vegetable exhales its strong savour. The atmosphere becomes impregnated, and the luscious qualities of the onion are wafted far and wide upon every passing breeze."

Farming in Connecticut (and presumably it was not very different in the upper reaches of the valley) was described in rather romanticized terms in the *Gazetteer:*

> The State of Connecticut is laid out in small farms from 50 to 300 and 400 acres each, which are held by the farmers in fee simple; and are generally well cultivated. The state is checkered with innumerable roads or highways crossing each other in every direction. A traveler in any of these roads, even in the most unsettled parts of the state, will seldom pass more than half a mile or a mile without finding a house, and a farm, under such improvements, as to afford the necessaries for the support of a family. The whole state resembles a well cultivated garden, which, with that degree of industry that is necessary to happiness, produces the necessaries and conveniences of life in great plenty.
>
> The farmers in Connecticut, and their families, are mostly clothed in plain, decent, homespun cloth. Their linens and woollens, are manufactured in the family way; and although they are generally of a coarser kind, they are of a stronger texture, and much more durable than those imported from France and Great-Britain. Many of their cloths are fine and handsome. Here are large orchards of mulberry trees; and silk worms have been reared to successfully, as to promise not only a supply of silk to the inhabitants, but a surplusage for exportation.
>
> Their farms furnish them with all the necessaries, most of the conveniences, and but few of the luxuries of life. They, of course, must be generally temperate; and, if they choose, can subsist with as much independence as is consistent with happiness. The subsistance of the farmer is substantial, and does not depend on incidental circumstances, like that of most other professions. There is no necessity of serving an apprenticeship to the business, not of a large stock of money to commence it to advantage. Farmers, who deal much in barter, have less need of money than any other class of people. The ease with which a comfortable subsistence is obtained induces the husbandman to marry young. The cultivation of his farm makes him strong and healthful. He toils cheerfully through the day; eats the fruit of his own labor with a gladsome heart; at night devoutly thanks his bounteous God for his daily blessing; retires to rest, and his sleep is sweet.

Today, we have to assume that Jedidiah Morse had written this section of his *Gazetteer* several years before it was published in 1810, for the happy state of affairs he described had already deteriorated.

As in the prior century, America was not immune from the turmoils and rivalries of Europe. In the course of the conflict against Napoleon, Britain began to interfere with American shipping, seizing merchantmen and their cargoes in the Caribbean and impressing American seamen into the royal navy. Relations deteriorated, and Jefferson and Congress imposed the Embargo Act of 1807, prohibiting all exports out of the United States and forbidding American vessels to go to foreign ports.

The Embargo, enacted to deal a blow to Britain, had a devastating effect on American foreign trade. Ships were detained in harbors, and the coastal trade was stringently regulated. Connecticut exports fell from $1,625,000 in 1807 to $414,000 in 1808. Middletown exports were down from $85,000 in 1807 to $49,000 in 1810. Connecticut shipmasters could agree with the jingle written by a Massachusetts seafarer about the embargo:

> Our ships all in motion, Once whiten'd the ocean,
> They'd sail'd and return'd with their cargo;
> Now doom'd to decay, They have fallen a prey
> To Jefferson, Worms, and Embargo.

This reduction in shipping brought depressed farm prices, widespread unemployment, and general dissatisfaction with the Madison administration that continued the Jeffersonian Embargo in the form of the Nonintercourse Act.

Meanwhile, further recriminations with Britain ensued which, abetted by bungling diplomacy on both sides, culminated in the War of 1812, a war bitterly opposed in New England where three-quarters of American shipping was owned.

During what was called "Mr. Madison's War," Connecticut Governor Matthew Griswold refused to permit the Connecticut militia to participate in the invasion of Canada; the Assembly declared a Federal conscription law unconstitutional; and the Hartford Common Council passed a bill forbidding Federal recruiting. In Massachusetts, the governor refused to call the state militia into national service, and the lower house issued a manifesto opposing any volunteers for the Federal forces. The war was equally unpopular in the upper valley where there was a lucrative trade with Canada, much of which, including the selling of large supplies of beef to the British forces, continued throughout the war.

Early in the war, the British blockaded various sections of the American coast. In the spring of 1814, their blockade was extended to New England. Many privateers were built to run the blockade. A number of these were built along the Connecticut.

Early in the morning on April 8, 1814, British marines from the blockade squadron in Long Island Sound, entered the Connecticut River on six barges to "fire" American shipping. Finding Saybrook Fort unmanned, they proceeded to Essex. They occupied the town for some six hours and burned some twenty-three vessels. The ship, the *Osage*, was still on the stocks at a yard in North Cove when the British struck. In an attempt to save her, the blocks were knocked away and she was prematurely launched, but she finally burned to the water line. The British then escaped down river.

The losses incurred at Essex harbor amounted to some $200,000 (a substantial sum in those days). The burned vessels represented holdings of not only Essex families, but those of Middletown, Old Lyme, East Haddam, and New York.

Because of the war's unpopularity, the Federalists, who had voted against the war, gained electoral victories throughout New England. Official delegates from Connecticut, Massachusetts, Rhode Island, and some

Kipp Solwedell: *The Raid of Essex.* 1964. Connecticut River Foundation Museum. As recounted in the *Pease and Niles Gazetteer* published in 1819:

> This village is memorable from the attack made upon it by the British, during the late war, and the entire destruction of the shipping in the harbour, which seems to have been the object of their *friendly* visit. This event occurred on the 8th of April, (being Good Friday, and a public Fast day,) 1814. A detachment from the British blockading squadron, then lying off New-London, consisting of several hundred soldiers and marines, made an excursion up the river, in six large barges, with muffled oars, and arrived at the landing in this village, about 3 o'clock in the morning. About 270 men were immediately landed, who rushed into, and took possession of the village. The commanding officer informed the inhabitants, that his orders were to burn the shipping, but not to molest the citizens, unless they were attacked; in which case, he was ordered to destroy every house in the village. . . . They burned all the vessels in the harbour, amounting to 23, and valued, subsequently, at $200,000. They also destroyed or stove several hogsheads of rum, and carried off several thousand dollars worth of cordage.

representatives from Vermont and New Hampshire met at the Hartford Convention in 1815 and voted for substantial changes in the federal constitution amidst talk of secession. However, with Commodore Thomas Macdonough's victory on Lake Champlain and Jackson's rousing victory in the Battle of New Orleans, the war ended and a new American national spirit emerged. The Hartford Convention was soon forgotten, and the Federalists lost their influence in New England as elsewhere.

In 1818, they were voted out of office in Connecticut, and a constitutional convention was held in Hartford at which a new constitution was enacted to take the place of the Charter of 1662. Universal suffrage was

One of the leaders of the 1818 Convention was Oliver Wolcott, Jr., (1760-1833) of the Windsor Wolcotts. Originally a staunch Federalist who served as Washington's secretary of the Treasury, he later became a Republican (as the Jeffersonian party was then called) and served as governor of Connecticut from 1817 to 1827. He was the fourth man in his family to be Connecticut's governor. His grandfather, Roger, after serving as a major general in the Louisburg expedition of 1745, became governor from 1751 to 1754. Oliver's uncle, Matthew Griswold, was governor from 1784 to 1786. Oliver's father, Oliver, was a signer of the Declaration of Independence and governor from 1795 to 1797. In the words of Ellsworth Grant:

"What the Adamses were to Massachusetts the Wolcotts were to Connecticut, a family dynasty devoted to public service, the birth of the American republic and its preservation, and the husbandry of their family's reputation. Plain, frugal, industrious, temperate—these and like qualities stamped them as plodding aristocratic members of the Standing Order that ruled with a firm hand the affairs of colony, state and even nation. But they stood for more. Like other conservatives before and since who have occupied positions of power during times of crisis and change, they were forced by circumstances to break new ground and to initiate reforms whose time had come. They were, in a sense, revolutionary conservatives."

established, church and state were separated, and the entire tax system was revised.

Massachusetts, New Hampshire, and Vermont had "modernized" their constitutions many years before, but it was not until 1819 that New Hampshire passed a so-called toleration act to provide that nonmembers of the Congregational Church would not be taxed for its support. Indeed, it was only in 1876 that New Hampshire removed its requirement that representatives, senators, and the governor be of the Protestant religion.

In general, a new spirit of toleration was evidenced in religious matters during these years. Different groups were now made more welcome — Episcopalians, Catholics, and Baptists, among others. When the Shakers had established themselves in the 1780s, they had been met with hostile mobs, threats, arrests, and imprisonment, but by 1800, they had established nine communities in New England, two of which were in the river valley.

The Enfield, Connecticut, community was organized around 1780. It lasted until 1915 when the property was sold to the state for a prison farm. John Barber in his *Connecticut Historical Collections* of 1836 described these Shakers:

> The whole number of Shakers in this place is upwards of two hundred, who are divided into six families. The village is about five miles n.e. of the Congregational Church in Enfield. The religious tenets of the Shakers must of course necessarily affect the order of their societies, by producing an entire separation of the men from the women, and in this particular exhibit the only species of *Protestant monkery* in this country. Their buildings are remarkably neat and convenient, and every thing appears a model of neatness and economy. They are simple and plain in their manners; sober and industrious. The society in this place was established in 1780. There are perhaps about fifty buildings in the settlement, consisting of dwelling houses, workshops, storehouses, &c. They possess upwards of one thousand acres of a fine tract of land, in the northeast section of the town, which is under the highest degree of cultivation. Their improvements and attention to horticulture and gardening have rendered them the subjects of much commendation, and their garden seeds are justly celebrated. They also carry on various kinds of mechanical business, and their wares are much esteemed, being good and free from deception. They are, for their number, a wealthy and flourishing community.

The Enfield Shakers are credited with a "first" for the nation. Their garden seeds were sold in packages, as they are today, the first time this had ever been done.

The other Shaker community in the river valley was in Enfield, New Hampshire. At one point, the community extended over 3,000 acres and numbered 350 members. This Enfield group was particularly known for its textiles, linen, cotton, and wool. It was also distinguished for its buildings of granite, the most outstanding of which was the Church Family Dwelling House, built in 1837.

In 1848, the Shakers had built an extraordinary bridge one mile long, on floating logs. It saw its end in the hurricane of 1938, but, in 1940, a new bridge over Mascoma Lake was dedicated by the governor of New Hampshire in the presence of one of the last members of the Enfield Society, with a plaque reading as follows:

> Shaker Bridge Built by the Shakers in 1848. Was destroyed by hurricane in 1938. Rebuilt by the State Highway Department in 1940. Ded-

icated to the Shakers for their many services to the Town of Enfield, N. H. Truly Industrious — Always Helpful — A Kindly People.

This Enfield community lasted until 1918. Its buildings eventually were acquired by the LaSalette Fathers, and they are still used for religious purposes.

A different kind of community living developed in Putney, Vermont, as one of the first American utopian experiments. In 1839, John Humphrey Noyes, a former Congregational minister, established a community for communal living based on the principles and ideals of Plato. Initially, all material goods and labor were shared, but a few years later the sharing was extended to spouses under the name of "complex marriage." This was too much for the citizens of Putney and they forced out the community.

The end of the war also saw a renewal of the emphasis on the importance of education and higher learning. Education had always been a major concern of the early settlers, and even 180 years later, the river valley people felt the same way. They established a good number of respected and prestigious schools and colleges throughout the valley during these years. These included two preparatory schools, Haverhill Academy and Suffield Academy, both still in operation. Another preparatory school, the Hartford Female Seminary, was founded in 1823 to provide a liberal education for young women. Its founder was Catherine Beecher, the sister of Harriet Beecher Stowe. The school closed some years later.

A school for the deaf began in Hartford, due to the efforts of Dr. Mason Fitch Cogswell. Dr. Cogswell's daughter, Alice, was deaf, and there were no schools for the deaf in the country. Dr. Cogswell and other prominent Hartford citizens organized a drive to raise money to establish a school.

A front View of DARTMOUTH COLLEGE, with the CHAPEL & HALL.

Their monies helped send Dr. Thomas Gallaudet to Europe to learn how to educate the deaf. He returned with Laurent Clerc, an educator for the deaf, and in 1817, the Connecticut Asylum at Hartford for the Instruction of the Deaf opened. Today the school is the oldest school for the handicapped in the United States.

Four colleges were also established, that are still in existence today. Amherst College was founded in 1821 and was named after Lord Jeffrey Amherst, a commander of the British force in America in the last French and Indian War. Trinity College was founded two years later as the first Episcopal college in New England. Then called Washington College, it was located on the grounds of the present state capitol in Hartford, but was moved in 1872 to its present site.

Wesleyan University was established in 1830 in Middletown, which had long sought its own collegiate establishment. Middletown residents had tried to obtain Yale in 1716, and Washington College in 1824, but they had been unsuccessful. A few years later they made a site and buildings available to a small Vermont academy, but the academy preferred Vermont, leaving the buildings and grounds empty. At this time, the Methodist Church was seeking a location for its newly formed Wesleyan College. Different towns competed for the college, but the availability of the buildings and a contribution from the town resulted in the selection of Middletown.

Already in its forty-first year in 1810, Dartmouth College had become an important center for learning. Its student body was about the same size as those of Harvard, Yale, and Columbia, and larger than that of Princeton. The *American Gazetteer* of 1810 described Dartmouth of that time:

> "The number of undergraduates is, on the average, from 150 to 180 . . . The students are under the immediate government and instruction of a president, who is also professor of history, a professor of mathematics and natural philosophy, a professor of languages, and a professor of medicine and chemistry, and one tutor. The college is furnished with a handsome library, and a philosophical apparatus, tolerably complete. The buildings are a college of wood, 150 by 50 feet, and three stories high, containing thirty-six rooms for students. Also another large edifice, with a number of privileged rooms; a handsome chapel . . . . The situation is elevated, healthful and pleasant, commanding an extensive prospect to the W. A handsome Congregational meeting house, with a lofty spire, has lately been erected, in which the commencement exercises are exhibited. These fine buildings stand on a spacious square which is surrounded by a number of large and handsome dwelling houses; these and the houses which extend along the public roads which meet here, constitute one of the most pleasant and lively villages in New England."

Early in the century, the New Hampshire legislature attempted to make unilateral changes in the charter granted to Dartmouth. There ensued the famous Dartmouth College case in the Supreme Court which held that the charter was, in effect, a contract which the legislature could not change. The case was argued by Dartmouth alumnus Daniel Webster, who concluded his appeal with his famous entreaty that "it is . . . a small college, and yet there are those who love it."

Relations between Dartmouth and the state of New Hampshire were not of the closest. Hanover had been one of the sixteen New Hampshire towns that had preferred Vermont to New Hampshire. When Vermont reluctantly removed these towns from its jurisdiction, it continued to give Dartmouth state support and, even today, Dartmouth grants special scholarships to Vermont residents.

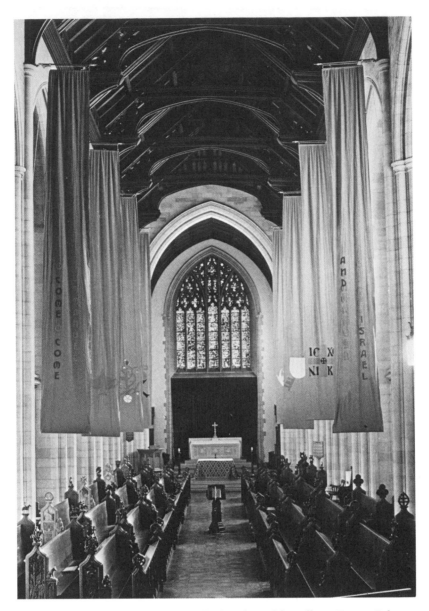

Built more than a hundred years after the founding of the college, Trinity College Chapel is a fine example of Gothic architecture. Designed by Frohman, Robb, and Little, architects of the National Cathedral in Washington, its tower of 163 feet contains a carillon of thirty bells.

Mount Holyoke, opened in 1837 by Mary Lyon as Mount Holyoke Female Seminary, marked the beginnings of college-level education for women. The objections raised to its establishment, as described some 50 years later by Amherst Professor William Tyler, seem utterly incredible in the world of coeducation as it exists today: "The objections to this idea of equalizing the educational advantages of the two sexes were many and various, and not always consonant with the courtesy due to the gentler sex. It was an innovation uncalled for, unheard of until now since the foundation of the world, and unthought of now except by a few strong-minded women and radical men, who would level all distinctions and overturn the foundations of the family, of society, of the church, and of the state. It was unnatural, unphilosophical, unscriptural, unpracticable, unfeminine and anti-Christian; in short all the epithets in the dictionary that begin with *un* and *in* and *anti* were hurled against and heaped upon it."

Great changes took place in the farmers' situation during these postwar years. All the bucolic sentiments expressed in the *Gazetteer* could not conceal the long hours of work, seven days a week with some limitations on the Sabbath, the inhospitable soil, and the long and dreary winters. To top it all off, there were some erratic summers like that of 1816 when frosts occurred every month in New Hampshire and Vermont, effectively killing all the crops and most of the livestock.

It was not long before farmers began to abandon their farms. As Samuel G. Goodrich wrote:

> The summer of 1816 was probably the coldest that has been known here, in this century. From Connecticut to Maine there were severe frosts in every month. I saw a man at Orford, N.H., who had been forty miles for a half bushel of Indian corn, and paid two dollars for it! At the same time, Ohio — with its rich soil, its mild climate, its inviting prairies — was open fully upon the alarmed and anxious vision. As was natural under the circumstances, a sort of stampede took place from cold, desolate, worn-out New England, to this land of promise. I remember very well the tide of emigration through Connecticut, on its way to the West, during the summer of 1817. Some persons went in covered wagons, some on foot and some crowded together under the cover, with kettles, gridirons, feather-beds, crockery, and the family

Lydia Huntley Sigourney (1791-1865) wrote more than fifty books and contributed more than 2,000 poems and articles to some 300 periodicals. Her home on Asylum Street in Hartford became the leading literary and social center of the first half of the nineteenth century.

A significant landmark of Hartford is the Wadsworth Atheneum, one of the oldest art museums in the United States. The original Gothic Revival building was designed by Ithiel Town and built in 1842. The subsequent addition of the Colt Memorial was built with funds from the widow of Samuel Colt, the Hartford firearms manufacturer, and the Morgan Memorial was donated by the elder J. Pierpoint Morgan, in memory of his father, a Hartford merchant.

Bible, Watts' *Psalms* and *Hymns*, and Webster's Spelling-book. I saw families on foot — father and boys taking turns dragging along an improvised handwagon, loaded with the wreck of the household goods — occasionally giving the mother and baby a ride.

With the opening of the Erie Canal in 1825, the emigration from all parts of New England increased dramatically. By 1860, Vermont had lost almost half of its population.

Many of those who emigrated were to distinguish themselves in the years to come. Salmon P. Chase left Cornish, New Hampshire, for Ohio, where he became governor and United States senator. He also served as secretary of the Treasury under Lincoln and chief justice of the Supreme Court. His uncle, Philander Chase, had founded an Episcopal Church in 1793, which still stands next to the Chase Homestead. Philander left New Hampshire for the midwest where he eventually became bishop of Ohio and Illinois. Morrison R. Waite, born in Lyme, Connecticut, and educated at Yale, emigrated to Ohio and later became chief justice of the Supreme Court.

(It may seem curious that four small Connecticut River towns produced four chief justices of the United States. In addition to Chase and Waite, Oliver Ellsworth, who was appointed by Washington, came from Windsor, Connecticut, and Harlan F. Stone, born in Chesterfield, New Hampshire, was appointed by Franklin D. Roosevelt. Perhaps, however, this was to be expected since the *American Gazetteer* of 1810 did note that "The people of Connecticut are remarkably fond of having all their differences settled according to law. The prevalence of this litigious spirit, affords employment and support for a numerous body of lawyers.")

Four sons and one daughter of David Dudley Field of Haddam also left Connecticut, and later they all achieved prominence. Field's son, David, was one of the most important American lawyers of his day and counsel to Samuel Tilden in the 1876 electoral controversy. His son, Stephen, became justice of the United States Supreme Court; Cyrus was the builder of the Atlantic Cable; and Henry was an author, journalist, and editor. Field's daughter, Emilia, was the mother of another Supreme Court justice, David J. Brewer, who sat on the court at the same time as his uncle.

Gradually subsistence farming disappeared, and by the middle of the century, agriculture in the valley was limited to certain specialized fields, such as livestock, horses, sheep, fruit, tobacco, onions, and dairy products.

Today's state animal of Vermont, the Morgan horse, descended from a famous Vermont progenitor, the famous Justin Morgan. Owned by various people in the Vermont and New Hampshire upper valley, Justin Morgan sired a considerable offspring before he died in 1821, and from these descended the famous breed of American light horses. Morgan horses, renowned for their strength and endurance, were used on cattle ranches, in the United States cavalry in the Civil War, to haul stages, and later to pull cars on New York's Sixth Avenue railroad.

Of particular interest in Bellows Falls is the Adams Old Stone Grist Mill Museum, with its fine collection of farm equipment and manufacturing artifacts typical of Vermont life in the nineteenth century. The mill was in operation from 1831 to 1861, processing cracked corn, grinding it into meal for household use and for animal feed at the rate of 10,000 bushels per day. Much of the original equipment is still intact and operable. The mill was about to be torn down in 1966, but the New England Power Company purchased its water rights and leased the mill to the Bellows Falls Historical Society.

Sheepraising assumed considerable importance in New England during the first half of the nineteenth century. David Humphreys, the American minister to Spain, returned from his Spanish post in 1802 with one hundred or more Merino sheep and set up a woolen mill in Seymour, Connecticut. A few years later William Jarvis, also an American diplomat, brought some 4,000 sheep from Spain to his farm at Weathersfield, Vermont. The Merino wool was far finer and richer than the wool then in use. The wool industry was considerably stimulated by the new breed, and new woolen mills were especially built to process the new wool. Sheepraising reached its peak between the 1830s and 1840s. By 1840, there were 2,250,000 Merino sheep in Vermont and New Hampshire, and the Merinos were the most important livestock in the area. The area prospered, as evidenced by the many beautiful, red brick homes built during these years which still grace the communities on both sides of the river.

Farms were not the only source of important products. The river, in addition to its role in the building and sailing of ships, represented an important economic resource on account of the abundance of its fish. The *American Gazetteer* of 1810 reported:

> Sturgeon, salmon, and shad, are caught in plenty in their season, from the mouth of the river upwards, excepting sturgeon, which do not ascend the upper falls; beside a variety of small fish, such as pike, carp, perch, &c.

William Jarvis was the first to introduce the Merino sheep to Vermont. He settled down on a huge estate in Weathersfield, where he built himself a mansion. Competition from the West and Australia eventually killed the New England wool industry, and Weathersfield Bow, which Jarvis had built up, became a deserted village.

GOLD DROP.

Salmon was abundant in the upper river:

> Notwithstanding the velocity of the current at Bellows Falls, above
> described, the salmon pass up the river, and are taken many miles
> above; but the shad proceed no farther. A canal is cut round these falls
> on the Vermont side. On the steep sides of the island and rock, at the
> fall, hang several arm chairs, secured by a counterpoise; in these the
> fishermen sit to catch salmon with fishing nets.

Connecticut River shad had always been considered to be among the
best, better, in the opinion of many, than the Hudson or Delaware shad.
The shad run was from April through mid-June. Fishing companies were
organized for the duration, hiring local farmers to work seven days a week
around the clock.

All along the river there were fish piers. Much of the shad was salted
and packed in barrels, and sent by ship to New York, Philadelphia, Baltimore, and the West Indies, but it was also eaten locally and used for fertilizer. Actually, shad was so abundant that farm hands insisted their job
contract include provisions limiting the number of times they could be
given shad as part of their meals.

This situation was to change dramatically during the second half of
the century because of the effects of the Industrial Age on the river.

7

THE INDUSTRIAL REVOLUTION

The importance of an internal supply of the first articles of necessity appears to be more understood and acknowledged every day . . . It may be asked, How long are we to continue thus like colonies dependent on a mother country? And will a period never arrive when it will be indispensable to clothe ourselves principally, with our own productions and fabrics?

David Humphreys
Founder of Humphreysville

The Industrial Revolution had begun. Humphreys was just one of many river valley inhabitants blessed with an inventive and self-reliant spirit, and an awareness of the value of the river and its tributaries. Jeremiah Wadsworth was another. The wealthiest man in Connecticut at the end of the Revolution, Wadsworth was continuously speculating in business enterprises. In 1789, he joined with Oliver Ellsworth and Governor Oliver Wolcott in the establishment of a woolen mill in Hartford. This was the first woolen mill in the country and was situated along the river, taking advantage of its water power. President Washington visited the "Woolen Manufactory at this place, which seems to be going on with spirit. Their Broadcloths are not of the first quality as yet, but they are good . . ." His diary notes that he ordered a suit which he wore when he delivered his message to Congress in 1790.

Unfortunately, the company lacked the know-how for wool operations and could not compete successfully with British imports, so it closed in 1795.

Other industries fared better. Seth Dexter opened a clothier works along the river near today's Windsor Locks in 1767, and later built a gristmill and sawmill in the same area. His grandson, who grew up in the business, discovered how to make wrapping paper from Manila rope. Today, producing specialty paper products, Dexter Corporation is the oldest manufacturing company in continuous existence in Connecticut.

Phineas Pratt began an ivory workshop in 1798 in an area of Essex (later to be called Ivoryton), utilizing ivory shipped from the ivory coast of Africa. Some years later, George Read and Phineas' son began an ivory comb business in Deep River. Eventually, in 1865, these operations and similar ivory businesses were merged to form Pratt, Read, and Company, the largest manufacturer of piano keys in the country today.

These were only the beginning. Notwithstanding the protests of New Englanders, the Embargo Act of 1807 and the War of 1812 had an unexpectedly favorable effect on the economy. Americans could not trade

J.W. Barber: *View of Hartford from the Eastern Bank of Connecticut River.*
About 1836.
   The first Hartford bridge across the Connecticut was built in 1810. After being washed away in 1818, it was succeeded by the covered bridge which can
be seen in the far right of this drawing. Burned in 1895, it was followed in
1908 by the Morgan Bulkeley Bridge.

abroad, but neither could English manufactured products get in. Ready
financing was available in America from the wealth which had been built
up by the shipping interests, and American industries expanded at a rapid
pace.
   By 1836, Hartford had become an important manufacturing center.
In the words of John Warner Barber in his *Connecticut Historical
Collections:*

> The manufactures of this city, by a late return made to the secretary of
> the treasury, exceed $900,000 per annum; among these are various
> manufactures of tin, copper and sheet iron; block tin and pewter ware;
> printing presses and ink; a manufactory of iron machinery; iron foun-
> daries; saddlery, carriages, joiners' tools, paperhangings, looking-
> glasses, umbrellas, stoneware, a brewery, a web manufactory, cabinet
> furniture, boots and shoes, hats, clothing for exportation, soap and can-
> dles, 2 manufactories of machine and other wire cards operated by
> dogs, &c, &c. More than twice as many books are published here an-
> nually, as are manufactured in any other place of equal population in
> the United States. There are 15 periodicals; 12 weekly newspapers, (5
> sectarian) 2 semi-monthly and 1 monthly.

These became the years of the Yankee peddler, who thrived mainly
because of the limited transportation facilities of the first half of the century. Initially on foot, then on horseback, and finally with horse and
wagon, the peddler plied the products of the Connecticut river valley
mills and factories up and down the Atlantic seaboard. He carried Noah
Webster's *Dictionary* from the Springfield publisher; ivory combs from
the Pratts; bells from Bell Town (East Hampton); elastic webbing from
Middletown's Russell Manufacturing Company; pewter from the Danforths in Rocky Hill — an incredible variety of wares.

91

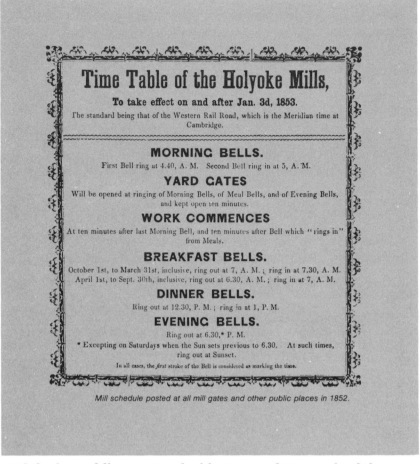

Time Table of the Holyoke Mills,

To take effect on and after Jan. 3d, 1853.

The standard being that of the Western Rail Road, which is the Meridian time at
Cambridge.

MORNING BELLS.

First Bell ring at 4.40, A. M.   Second Bell ring in at 5, A. M.

YARD GATES

Will be opened at ringing of Morning Bells, of Meal Bells, and of Evening Bells,
and kept open ten minutes.

WORK COMMENCES

At ten minutes after last Morning Bell, and ten minutes after Bell which "rings in"
from Meals.

BREAKFAST BELLS.

October 1st, to March 31st, inclusive, ring out at 7, A. M. ; ring in at 7.30, A. M.
April 1st, to Sept. 30th, inclusive, ring out at 6.30, A. M. ; ring in at 7, A. M.

DINNER BELLS.

Ring out at 12.30, P. M. ; ring in at 1, P. M.

EVENING BELLS.

Ring out at 6.30,* P. M.

* Excepting on Saturdays when the Sun sets previous to 6.30.   At such times,
ring out at Sunset.

In all cases, the *first* stroke of the Bell is considered as marking the time.

Mill schedule posted at all mill gates and other public places in 1852.

While the peddler was invaluable to manufacturers, he did not carry with him the best of reputations. British traveler, John Bernard, learned that the Southern businessman regarded the Northern peddler

> "in the light of a visitation," and looked upon a "Connecticut chap as a commercial Scythian, a Tartar of the North whose sole business in life is to make inroads on his peace and profit. He ranks him in the list of plagues next to the yellow fever, and before locusts, taxation, and a wet spring . . . . There is no getting rid of them. None of the usual similes of a burr, or sticking-plaster, give any idea of the pedlar's tenacity; he has the grip of a crab, with the suction of a mosquito; you can't deny, you can't insult, you can't fatigue him; you can only dismiss him with a purchase . . .

And purchase people did. With their products selling so well, businesses thrived, and more businesses began. All along the river and its tributaries, entrepreneurs were learning how to take advantage of all that free water power. That is what happened to Holyoke.

Holyoke has the distinction of being the first planned industrial community in America. In the 1840s, a group of Boston and New York investors observed that around Holyoke there was the perfect combination of a sixty-foot drop in the river at Hadley Falls, and a broad plain of farm land just below the falls. They reasoned that they could construct a dam across the river there and establish a number of textile mills on the land.

In 1848, they constructed what at that time was the largest dam in the world. The dam came to a disastrous end on the very day of its inauguration. As reported by the newly invented telegraph to its Boston sponsors:

10:00 A.M.	— Gates just closed; water filling behind dam.
12:00 NOON	— Dam leaking badly.
2:00 P.M.	— Stones of bulkhead giving way to pressure.
3:20 P.M.	— Your old dam's gone to Hell by way of Willimansett.

Another dam was built the next year, with a series of canals to channel the water to the mills. Eventually three canals were built, with a whole series of mills along the canal banks. The mills all used and re-used the same water as it passed from one to another. The mills later turned into paper mills, and for years Holyoke was the leading manufacturing center in the United States for writing paper and envelopes.

Chester, halfway between the river mouth and Middletown, provides an interesting contrast to Holyoke. Typical of the many smaller towns along the river, Chester was fortunate to have two streams flowing through town. Small dams were built along them to back up the water into little ponds, with the flow being diverted to factories.

Taking advantage of the abundance of this water power, over fifty small factories were in operation in Chester during most of the nineteenth century, producing such varied products as wood screws, gimlets, bits,

The Holyoke Dam, on the far right, and the three Holyoke canals as they appear today.

brushes, augers, axe handles, small tools, Brittania ware, and Silliman ink-wells used in "portable ink stands" by armies in the field during the Civil War.

The most important contribution of the Connecticut River valley industry was the development of interchangeable parts which were produced by elaborate machine tools. Their use led to the development of the machine tool and small arms industry in Middletown; Hartford; Springfield, Massachusetts; and Windsor, Vermont.

In Middletown, Simeon North operated a pistol factory with a government contract dating from 1799. He was one of the first to produce interchangeable parts through mass production. By 1853, his factory had produced 50,000 pistols and 33,000 rifles. In 1846, the Robbins and Law-

Gladding's Brush Factory in Chester, dating from about 1834, was one of over fifty small factories in operation in Chester in the nineteenth century. Almost all of these have disappeared, but this factory has been preserved and re-adapted for use as the Chart House Restaurant. The covered bridge over the creek was added in 1971.

Windsor, Vermont, has a long and important industrial history as an early home of the machine tool industry. Its contributions in this field are memorialized in the American Precision Museum that houses a major collection of hand and machine tools and their products, such as a steam engine, electrical generator, sewing machines, and typewriters. The three-story museum was built in 1846 by Robbins and Lawrence as an armory and machine shop. After the Civil War, production centered on tools and products for the civilian market until 1872 when the building became a cotton mill and subsequently a hydroelectric power station.

rence Armory was established in Windsor, Vermont, with machinery to make army rifles with interchangeable parts. After seeing its machinery at the Crystal Palace Industrial Exhibition in London in 1851, a British parliamentary commission came to Windsor to study the details of the "American System" and ordered special machines to be shipped to British arsenals.

During the Civil War, Connecticut River valley industries were important suppliers of arms for the Union forces. Colt's Armory in Hartford produced 387,000 revolvers, 6,693 rifles, and 113,900 muskets. Christian Sharps' Rifle Manufacturing Company, also in Hartford, turned out some 33,000 rifles yearly. The Springfield Armory was equally busy. In 1864, its production reached 1,000 rifles a day, with over 3,000 people employed. Of equal importance to the Union forces was the large supply of gunpowder from Colonel Augustus Hazard's Powder Company in Enfield.

After the Civil War, the arms industry declined and many of the arms factories were turned to other uses, such as machine tools and metal components.

Other thriving river valley enterprises during the nineteenth century were logging and quarrying. Lumber had been one of the most important

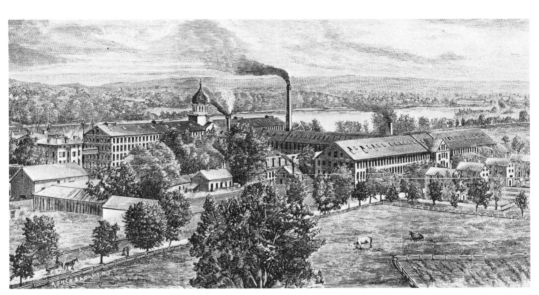

The most prominent nineteenth century industrialist in Hartford was undoubtedly Samuel Colt, one of America's most successful inventors. Colt thought up his famous "six-shooter" around 1830 and later persuaded the military of its usefulness. He sold a large quantity of his revolvers to the government during the Mexican War, and then established an armory in Hartford in 1854. In the southern meadows along the river, he built his armory with a large, blue, onion-shaped dome and topped with a golden ball and a bronze colt holding a broken spear. Surrounding the armory were multiple dwellings for his employees and their families. The entire project was protected from river floodings by a series of privately built dikes. Although Colt died prematurely at the age of 47, the Colt Armory continued and eventually became part of Colt Industries.

exports from the upper valley since early Colonial days. The forests of New Hampshire and Vermont, which bordered on the river and its tributaries, afforded an almost unending supply of fine wood. Indeed, in the early New Hampshire grants, the great pine trees were specifically reserved for use in the King's navy.

The Revolution brought an end to the restrictions of the so-called Pine Laws, and logging became a free-for-all. The upper reaches of the river were opened up, and timber cutting reached the very sources of the river along the Canadian border. Many sawmills were established along the river, one of the most important being the one at the foot of Mount Tom on the Oxbow loop near Northampton. During the winter, logs were cut, fashioned together in a "box," and tied together into huge rafts. After the spring thaw, these were floated down the river to the sawmills, being disassembled whenever necessary to bypass the rapids or the falls, or to pass through the locks at Bellows Falls.

In the lower valley, where the river flows through rock ledges, it was natural that large deposits of rock would be available for quarrying. Deep River began quarrying in 1812, and the products of its eight quarries were shipped to New York and Philadelphia, where there was a great demand for building stone and paving blocks.

Portland for many years was the principal source of Connecticut brownstone. Special barges were built in Lyme to float it down the river to New York and Philadelphia all during the nineteenth century. Row after row of identically designed brownstone buildings in these cities, plus the Vanderbilt and Gallatin mansions on New York's Fifth Avenue and the Union League Club in Philadelphia, were built with Portland brown-

The Springfield Arsenal of 1778 became a federal armory in 1794. The site was personally selected by President Washington and General Henry Knox, the Secretary of War, who, coincidentally, happened to live in Springfield. During the Civil War, the armory provided some 800,000 rifles. The Springfield Rifle, invented in 1903, was used in World War I. World War II and the Korean War saw the Garand Rifle, invented in 1937, of which Springfield produced four and a half million of the total production of six million. The last of the Springfields was the MI4 Automatic Rifle used in Vietnam. Closed in 1968, the extensive facilities of the arsenal have been converted into the Springfield Technical Community College with some 5,000 students. There remains an armory museum with a fascinating collection of small arms with the huge rifle storage racks where, in the words of Henry Wadsworth Longfellow, "from floor to ceiling, like a huge organ, rise the burnished arms."

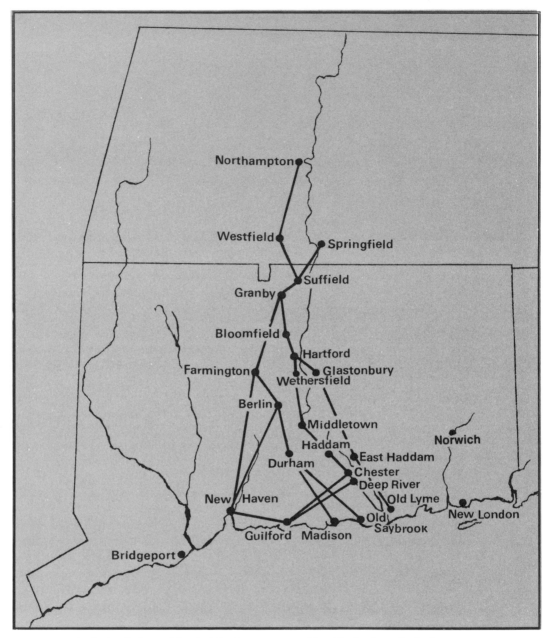

As the birthplace of the abolitionist movement, New England was in the fore-
front of the anti-slavery movement. The Connecticut River valley played an
important part in the Underground Railroad, with stations hidden in towns all
along the river. Runaway slaves were often carried upriver on the many boats
plying the river. The Nook Farm Complex in Hartford, where the Mark Twain
Memorial and Harriet Beecher Stowe house are found today, was an important station on the Underground Railroad. It was owned by Senator Francis
Gillette, a leading abolitionist. Springfield was another important station on
the Underground Railroad. John Brown, later to be hanged after the Harpers
Ferry raid, was an active abolitionist in Springfield for several years where he
operated a wool warehouse. By 1848, slavery had been abolished in all of
New England (it had never been recognized in Vermont). And yet, along the
lower river towns were iron forges where shackles were made and shipped
south.

The life of the logman was a rough one, as Samuel G. Goodrich noted in the 1840s:

> "The lumberer or river drivers often earn five or six dollars a day, but no course of life is attended with greater hardships, and nothing can be more destructive to health and morals. To stimulate the frame and enable it to endure the toil and exposure, these men take immoderate quantities of ardent spirits, and habits of intemperance are the consequence. Premature old age, and shortness of days are too frequently the fate of a lumberer. The money they so laboriously earn, is spent with a thoughtless extravagance. After selling and delivering their timber, they pass some weeks in idle indulgence."

stone. Shipments were even sent around Cape Horn for a house being built in San Francisco.

Brownstone also came from a quarry owned by the Shailer family in Haddam. Surrounding the quarry was a specially built village, called Shailerville. This was one of over 200 "-villes" in Connecticut during the nineteenth century. "-Villes" were built to provide a self-sufficient community for the laborers at the mill or factory at their center. The mill or factory owner built houses, schools, churches, and stores in his community. This was in an attempt to attract labor, including child labor, by providing a respectable environment, a modest education, a moral upbringing, and strict discipline. Adult work involved a twelve-hour day, six days a week, and monthly wages.

Besides Shailerville, there were several other "-villes" directly in the river valley. Laysville was established in Old Lyme around the Lay woolen factory, and Johnsonville was in East Haddam around Emory Johnson's twine mill. Today, Johnsonville is a recreated village privately owned, open to the public only occasionally. Included in the village is a mill office, a general store, a period home, a schoolhouse, a chapel, and a livery stable with an antique carriage collection. On the mill pond is a dam, sawmill, and covered bridge, along with a small steamwheeler reminiscent of old steamboat days.

One adverse effect of the Industrial Age was felt by the shad fishing industry. The construction of the Holyoke Dam in 1849 eventually blocked the spawning of the fish, and shad began to be in short supply. In 1867, however, a fish culturist began the breeding of shad under artificial conditions at Holyoke and planted the eggs in the river. These efforts resulted in record catches for a while during the 1870s. In one day, over 28,000 shad were taken in Saybrook alone.

However, the day of the decline of shad fishing had set in. As factories and population increased, the river became increasingly polluted. Despite attempts to breed fish in special ponds, the operations of organized fish companies ceased, and shad fishing became one or two-man operations. By the end of the century, the days of large scale fishing had passed.

The salmon fared even worse and were doomed when mill dams were built along the river's tributaries, blocking the route to spawning grounds.

In light of the importance of the river as an avenue of commerce and of Connecticut's long seafaring tradition, it was obvious that shipbuilding should become one of the most important industries along the navigable part of the river. Thomas A. Stevens has estimated that the Connecticut River shipyards produced over 4,000 vessels during the nineteenth century.

The shipyards in Essex and Portland were the most important. Essex had eight yards, a rope walk, two block and spar shops, two sail lofts, ship chandleries, and warehouses. Over 500 vessels were built in the Hayden, Scovill, Williams, and Starkey shipyards. The largest ship launched was the *Middlesex* in 1851, of 1,426 tons.

The Gildersleeve yards in Portland, which operated from 1741 down to 1930, produced the *Trumbull* of 700 tons during the Revolution and the gun boat, *Cayuga*, of 1600 tons in 1864. Sailing vessels, steamships, and warships were also produced at this yard, including most of the ships for the line between New York and Galveston established in 1836.

Smaller shipyards were found all along the river. Some 200 vessels were launched in Lyme from four different shipyards. The oldest, established before the Revolution, was the Hill Yard on the Lieutenant River where brigs and schooners of up to 290 tons were produced. Brockway's Shipyard on the Connecticut itself built vessels in the 1820s for the Stonington Antarctic Sealing Trade. The largest vessel produced in Lyme was the 633-ton *Grace Seymour*, launched in 1888.

The East Haddam shipyards of the Greenes, Warners, Haydens, and Goodspeeds, accounted for over 400 ships. At the Goodspeeds' yard, sailing ships and steamboats were built. With the onset of the Civil War, the yard turned to the building of warships and gun boats, the best known of which was then *U.S.S. Kanawha* which was built and delivered in ninety days.

In Middle Haddam, Thomas Child's yards built 237 vessels, including the first Connecticut ships for the China trade, as well as several of the

Captain Henry L. Champlin was pioneer shipmaster of John Griswold's New York to New London line. Champlin's wife, the daughter of Uriah Hayden of Essex, accompanied him on many of his voyages. Their three children were born at sea. Champlin retired to Essex in 1840 and lived at Champlin Square with his family.

first London packets. The shipyards along the river were substantial enterprises. In addition to the building and repair of the actual vessels, the larger shipyards maintained ships' stores and chandleries and employed many chandlers, carpenters, riggers, spar- and blockmakers, chainforgers, caulkers, ropewalkers, sawmill workers, and sailmakers. Many shipyard owners were also shipmasters and successful merchants.

These shipmasters were perhaps even more significant to the Connecticut River valley than the shipbuilders. In his *Connecticut River Master Mariners*, Thomas Stevens describes shipmasters from that time "when ships were made of wood and men of iron":

> No part of New England produced a finer group of shipmasters than those men whose home towns bordered the Connecticut River. These River Towns contributed no less than a thousand captains—many of whom were of world renown—whose exploits and records remain unsurpassed. It is almost impossible to mention more than a few without overlooking many more that were equally important. Every River Town is represented by native sons whose names are high in the maritime profession of the last century. Many were better known in London, Liverpool, or the Far East, than at home. On the front page of the *New York Post* of the 1840's can be found the names of at least thirty Commanders of the finest New York ships afloat whose homes had been built in the lower Connecticut River Valley . . . .

101

While in China, Samuel Russell drew up plans for a house to be built for him on High Street in Middletown. He hired Ithiel Town to be the architect, and the house was completed in 1830. The garden and grounds covered more than five acres, all beautifully landscaped with boxwood, potted trees, pomegranates, and other shrubs. The house was considered the showplace of Middletown. Many famous guests were entertained in the mansion. In 1859, Edward Everett, the most famous orator of the time and one-time president of Harvard and secretary of state, visited Middletown to give for the 109th time his lecture on George Washington. He stayed at the Russell house and wrote his wife that "nothing could exceed the luxury of my quarters" at the "Russell Palace." In 1936, the mansion was presented to Wesleyan University.

Samuel Mather of Deep River was one of America's leading shipmasters. He captained the famous clipper ship, the *Nightingale*, which made new records for speed. During the Civil War, the Union Defense Committee recognized Mather's achievements and appointed him to command the *U.S.S. Henry Andrews*. He was killed in action in 1862 at the age of 38 while in command of his ship in Florida and was buried in Deep River.

Also from the lower river valley came many of the great shipping merchants who owned fleets of vessels. John Griswold of Old Lyme pioneered the Black X London Line which gave the first London-New York schedule of regular packet ships in 1824. Nathaniel L. and George Griswold, also of Lyme, began business as brokers for ships built along the river. Their firm became one of the most important shippers in the China trade with the largest and fastest sailing vessels of the day. Another famous name in the China trade was Samuel Russell of Middletown, the founder of Russell and Company of Canton, China. He also owned the Russell Manufacturing Company in Middletown that made woven elastic webbing.

Along with the growth of the shipping industry came the growth of the insurance business, always important in the spreading of risk so that no individual has to bear an entire loss. An important shipping center since the Revolution, Hartford naturally became involved in the insurance business. Marine insurance was followed by fire and casualty insurance. The Hartford Fire Insurance Company was incorporated in 1810, followed by Aetna in 1819.

These companies were managed with good Yankee prudence by businessmen of principle as well as ability. The great test came with the December, 1834, fire in New York City. Having little information about the extent of the losses covered by his company, Hartford Fire Insurance Company's president, Eliphalet Terry, called the Hartford banks for assurances of support, pledging his own personal fortune. He immediately proceeded to New York by sleigh. When he arrived, he found that most of the New York companies had been bankrupted by the losses, and he publicly announced that his company would pay all claims in full. The company was then immediately overwhelmed with new business, and Hartford's reputation as the insurance capital of the world dates from this incident.

And yet another important activity was born on the Connecticut River during these years — the steamboat.

8

THE STEAMBOAT ERA BEGINS

The first successful steamboat was put in operation on the Hudson in
the year 1807, it being the acknowledged invention of Robert Fulton . . .
An experiment had been made, with the steam engine, on the Seine,
near Paris, in 1803; but no vessel was set in motion by steam, in the
United States, till four years afterward.

— *S.G. Goodrich, A Pictorial History of the*
United States for the Use of Schools and Families
Philadelphia, 1870

And so were taught American children in the nineteenth century. In actual fact, Fulton was not the inventor of the steamboat. The first successful
operation of a steamboat was by John Fitch, who had been born in Windsor, Connecticut. His steamboat, in 1787, carried thirty passengers twenty
miles upstream on the Delaware River. Five years later, Samuel Morey of
Orford, New Hampshire, successfully ran his steamboat, the *Aunt Sally*,
on the upper Connecticut River between Orford and Fairlee, Vermont.
Several years later Morey built a stern-wheeler in New York which made
the 150-mile trip to Hartford, the longest steamboat trip which had ever
been made until then. A year later he received a patent on his engine,
signed by George Washington.

Morey, however, lacked the finances to make his steamboat a profitable venture. He gave his designs to New York Chancellor Robert Livingston, hoping to secure financing for his project. Livingston made them
available to Fulton, who then based the *Clermont* on Morey's designs.
Morey, not without considerable justification, believed himself the vic-
tim of duplicity and theft. (In spite of this setback, Morey pursued his
inventive career, receiving, all in all, twenty different patents over a period of forty years.)

Thus, the steamboat was invented by Connecticut River people, but
Fulton is the man who gets the credit for convincing the public of the
practicability of steamboat navigation.

The first commercial steamboat service on the Connecticut began in
1813 with the *Julianna*, which ran between Middletown and Hartford.
The boat left Hartford at eight A.M. and arrived at Middletown three hours
later, with the return trip taking four and one-half hours. For whatever
reason, the venture was not a success and was soon discontinued.

In 1815, steamboat service was established between New York and
New Haven with the *Fulton*. This boat was 134 feet long and carried a full
set of sails to be used in an emergency. In May of that year, the *Fulton*

Oliver Ellsworth, Mariners Museum.
"The steamboat *Oliver Ellsworth* is 112 feet keel, 24 feet beam, and 8 feet hold, measuring nearly 230 tons — length of deck 127 feet and 36 feet in width to the outside of the guards — is covered from the wheels aft with a tight roof or promenade deck 60 feet in length, surrounded with substantial railing — has a gentlemen's cabin forward about 24 feet in length, containing 16 births, a dining cabin 54 feet in length containing 30 births, and a ladies cabin on deck 26 feet in length, containing 16 births, together with state rooms, offices, baggage rooms, &c. &c. She was built by Messrs. Isaac Webb & Co. of this city (New York) — the engine, which is of the power of 44 horses, and of first rate workmanship, was constructed by Mr. James P. Allaire. The boat is commanded by Capt. Daniel Havens, a gentleman of experience in the carrying of passengers and navigating the sound. It is expected that this boat will be connected with the new steamboat *Henry Eckford,* which will soon commence running between this city and Norwich, by which arrangement, and the aid of a branch boat from the mouth of the Connecticut, eight trips per week can be made between this city and the towns situated upon the Thames and Connecticut Rivers . . ."
New York *Daily Advertiser*

made a side trip to Saybrook and then to Hartford. As reported in the Connecticut *Courant:*

> On Thursday morning, the inhabitants of this town, and the people, collected on account of the Election, were gratified by the arrival in the river opposite the city, of the elegant Steam-Boat Fulton, which regularly plies between New-York and New-Haven, with a load of passengers from those places. The novelty and elegance of this vessel, attracted universal attention, and it is supposed, that on that day and the next morning, not less than seven or eight thousand persons were on board of her, who were treated with great attention and respect by Captain Bunker. On Friday she went down the river with a great number of passengers, for the purpose of making her accustomed trip from New-Haven to New-York on Saturday.

In 1822, William C. Redfield of Cromwell, Connecticut, incorporated the Connecticut Steamboat Company. Redfield, besides being an early pioneer in the development of steamboat navigation on the river, also was known in meteorological circles for his studies on the rotary motions of storms. His company introduced a sixty-two ton sidewheeler, the *Experiment,* for biweekly trips between Hartford and Essex. The Essex landing was at Captain Timothy Starkey's wharf at the foot of Main Street.

Redfield's company also had the Isaac Webb company of New York build the *Oliver Ellsworth* for a regular run from Hartford to New York. This vessel was the first yet seen on the river with separate cabins for ladies and gentlemen, staterooms, and other niceties of travel.

During these years, the Fulton-Livingston monopoly on New York waters prevented the Connecticut River steamboats from direct access to New York. Passengers had to disembark near Greenwich for a twenty-five mile stagecoach ride into the city. In 1825, the United States Supreme Court ruled that the monopoly was an invalid restraint on commerce, thus opening the port of New York to all.

Business soon became highly profitable, and the Hartford Steamboat Company entered the field with the *Macdonough* of 273 tons and 132 feet. At first, it was a rival of the Connecticut Steamboat Company. Soon, however, the two companies decided to share the route by staggering their schedules. The *Ellsworth* left Hartford on Mondays and Thursdays, and the *Macdonough* left on Wednesdays and Saturdays. The 150-mile trip to New York cost five dollars and took approximately fifteen hours with an average speed of ten knots.

The *Macdonough* was larger than the *Ellsworth,* with berths for seventy-six passengers, and also had a covered freight room. A contemporary description in New York newspapers described her interior arrangements:

> The furniture throughout is of the best order, fine hair mattresses, Marseilles quilts, and (what is most comfortable) wide as well as good linen. The ladies cabin is furnished with two handsome work tables, and with ten mahogany, hair-bottom sofas, permanently fixed in front of the births. Both the cabins are well lighted and ventilated, and no pains have been spared to make her a safe, pleasant, and comfortable boat. The engine and machinery, which are strong and powerful, were made by George Birbec & Co. of this city.

The *Ellsworth* and the *Macdonough* stopped at a number of landings along the river. As well as taking valley residents on excursions "upon the salt water" to the "city of New York, passing in view of the Navy Yard, fortifications, various islands, etc.,'' the boats provided them with special excursions to parades and exhibitions in different towns.

On one excursion, several miles out of Saybrook, the *Ellsworth*'s boiler ruptured, killing a fireman and injuring a few passengers. Having no steam, she hoisted sail and returned to Saybrook. When the damage had been repaired, she re-entered service with the improvements described in the *Courant:*

> Oliver Ellsworth, — This boat, having undergone the repairs rendered necessary by the melancholy accident of last Spring, has resumed her regular trips between this city and New York. She has been furnished with a new copper boiler, and every exertion seems to have been made to secure safety to the passengers. The boiler contains 28,000 lbs. of sheet and bolt copper, and each sheet is braced to prevent bursting or collapsing.
>
> It is pronounced by those who have seen it, a superior specimen of strength, workmanship and design. The plan is upon the *low pressure* principle, similar to the boiler in the New Philadelphia, on the North River. In addition to every ordinary precaution, a glass tube is inserted so as to show to the engineer and passengers, the precise height of water in the boiler.

Passenger and freight service on the Hartford to New York run proved so highly lucrative with the *Ellsworth* and the *Macdonough* that it was not long before competition came in to challenge them. One competitor was the *Victory*, a 290-tonner previously on the Hudson River service. Its arrival sparked a vigorous price war, abetted by a war of words. The old-timers were backed by newspaper editorials lauding the "safe and responsible line of boats" as against "transient and insecure accommodations" of the newcomers. The owners of *Victory* replied in a public advertisement:

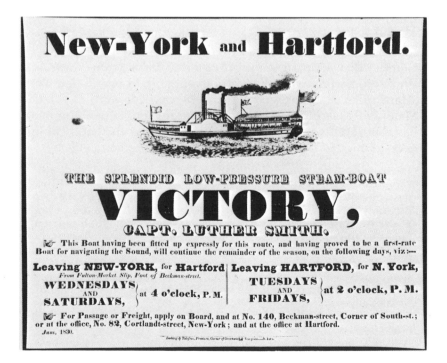

... The Victory was not placed on this route with a view to prejudice the interest of the old companies, she occupied the vacant days of the week, put the fare at a reasonable rate, at a rate which would enable boats to make a fair profit, and ensure the public an elegant, safe and expeditious passage between New York and Hartford. Let the public here remark the conduct of the old companies — as soon as the Victory came on, *their* fare was reduced at once from the moderate sum of FIVE DOLLARS — to the more moderate sum of $1.50, meals to be paid for in addition, to be sure — not succeeding in this effort, they have at length magnanimously raised *their* fare the sum of 50 cents — and constituted what they call a daily line with the old boats, one of which is to leave on the same day of the Victory, in the hope of compelling the Victory to withdraw from the route; and the present arrangement . . . is entered into without a "special regard to the due observance of the Sabbath."

The *Victory* was sold in 1833, and *Macdonough* was supplanted in 1833 by the *New England* of 261 tons and 153 feet. The *New England* had "two copper boilers of great strength," unfortunately not great enough to withstand an explosion on the morning of October 9, 1833, while anchored off Essex. Fifteen of her seventy passengers were killed or injured.

Notwithstanding this disaster and reports of similar disasters, either by explosion or fire or foul weather, steamboat navigation continued to develop amidst increasing competition. Commodore Cornelius Vanderbilt, who had achieved considerable success on the Hudson River, pitted his *Water Witch* against the *New England* in 1833, making the passage between Hartford and New York in thirteen hours. The *Water Witch* was replaced two years later by the *Lexington*, 488 tons and 207 feet long, and the fastest steamboat of the day. The *Hartford Times* commented:

> ... The *Lexington* has since her first trip been almost as regular as the sun, and as yet has never lost a trip, and very seldom been an hour behind her regular time, never met with the slightest accident; blow high, blow low, fair or foul, sunshine or fog . . . .

This was the same *Lexington* which caught fire off Fishers Island on January 13, 1840, and sank, with a loss of 150 lives.

Competition with Vanderbilt resulted in further price wars and the fare dropped, first to two dollars and eventually to one dollar. The fare from Hartford to Saybrook went down to twenty-five cents.

Meanwhile, the *Bunker Hill* was brought into service by the Connecticut interests, which Vanderbilt countered with the *Cleopatra* in 1836. Again, the *Hartford Times* gave a glowing report:

> We were highly gratified . . . in visiting the new steamboat *Cleopatra*, Capt. Reynolds, on her first trip from New York. This splendid Boat has been built expressly for the route . . . and together with the *Lexington* will form a daily *regular* line, second to no line in the United States — consequently in the world. The symmetry and elegance of model — the strength and substantialness of the work, the perfect finish of the mechanical work of her Hull and engine, the magnificent furnishing and fitting up of the cabins, and the almost incredible speed of these boats, altogether combine to render them the most perfect specimens of naval architecture ever produced; and which almost bid defiance to all competition . . . .
> The *Cleopatra* is fitted with her boilers on her guards, has an engine of about four feet cylinder, and eleven feet stroke of piston, is remarkably stiff, her forward and after cabins are connected and magnificently

The sinking of the Lexington was portrayed by Currier and Ives in a vividly realistic print showing the flaming vessel and its frenzied passengers desperately seeking to survive. The print was captioned "AWFUL CONFLAGRATION OF THE STEAM BOAT LEXINGTON ON LONG ISLAND SOUND ON MONDAY EVE'G. JAN'Y 13th 1840, BY WHICH MELANCHOLY OCCURRENCE OVER 100 PERSONS PERISHED." The *Lexington* print, published only three days after the disaster, was the first great Currier and Ives best seller and marked the beginning of the use of prints as a means of mass journalistic reporting.

fitted up, she makes up 180 sleeping berths, and altogether appears quite comfortable. — We trust that the travelling community will patronize her as she shall merit.

Not to be outdone, the Connecticut River Steamboat Company came up with the *Charter Oak* as described in the *Courant:*

The Connecticut River Steam Boat Company have built a new Steam Boat, which is now at New York for the purpose of taking in her engine . . . . We had an opportunity to examine it . . . and . . . we have no doubt she will prove to be a first rate vessel. She is about 200 feet long, 50 feet wide, 25 feet beam, and 9 feet 6 inches deep, and her tonnage is about 500 tons. The gentlemen's cabin extends the whole length of the boat, and contains 150 births. The ladies' cabin is 16 feet wide, and contains 36 births; and in both there is ample space for extra births when necessary. Both the cabins are fine lofty rooms. The promenade deck is 150 feet in length. The main deck, when finished, will be entirely shielded from the weather.

Steamboat travel on the upper Connecticut River was another matter. The Enfield, Connecticut, rapids were the principal obstacle to river traffic north of Hartford. Only flatboats carrying less than ten tons could be poled up the rapids. Cargoes on larger boats had to be transferred to ox

CONNECTICUT RIVER STEAMBOATS

Name	Date	Tonnage	Destiny
Bunker Hill	1835	310	On Saybrook rocks 1852
Charter Oak	1837	439	Burned New York 1850
Chief Justice Marshall	1825	314	Lost 1835
City of Hartford	1852	814	Lost off Rye 1886
City of Lawrence	1867	1678	Lost off Block Island 1907
City of Richmond	1880	614	Burned 1904
Cleopatra	1836	402	Last reported 1862
Commerce	1825	271	Scrapped 1893
Connecticut	1848	1129	Boiler explosion 1890
Cricket	1846	204	Sunk Hudson River 1894
Enterprize	1819	105	Last reported 1823
Experiment	1822	62	Last reported 1828
Globe	1842	481	Lost off Texas 1851
Granite State	1853	887	Burned East Haddam 1883
Hartford	1892	1338	Last reported 1936
Hartford	1899	1488	Scrapped 1938
Hero	1845	462	Sold abroad 1870
Kosciusko	1839	250	Converted to barge
Lexington	1835	488	Burned off Long Island 1840
Macdonough	1826	272	Lost off New Jersey 1839
Mary Benton	1861	365	Scrapped 1897
Middletown	1896	1554	Scrapped 1938
New Champion	1841	381	Last reported 1887
New England	1833	261	Sunk off Maine 1838
Oliver Ellsworth	1824	227	Last reported 1853
Silver Star	1864	202	Burned 1902
Splendid	1832	209	Stranded and lost 1856
State of New York renamed City of Springfield	1867	1417	Last reported 1905
Sunshine	1864	420	Last reported 1894
Victory	1827	290	Lost 1894
Washington Irving	1844	149	Last reported 1868
Water Witch	1831	207	Last reported 1862

The list of the larger steamboats in service on the river was compiled from a more detailed list appearing in *The Connecticut River Steamboat Story* by Melancthon W. Jacobus

carts, driven to Thompsonville, and then reloaded on flatboats to reach the upper river. North of Enfield, canals had been constructed to bypass river obstructions at South Hadley, Turners Falls, Bellows Falls, Hartland, and Wilder, but these canals were short in length and quite narrow. They had been built mainly to facilitate rafts and flatbottomed boats, and no steamboat that existed up to this time could get through them. With problems like these, it is not surprising that not much was done to push steamboat navigation on the upper river in the early years of steamboat travel. However, that situation was to change in the 1820s.

New Haven merchants had long been jealous of the Connecticut River traffic which had made Hartford an important port. They also were impressed by the success of the Erie, Chesapeake, and Ohio canals which proved that people infinitely preferred the comfort of a trip by canal over a trip by stagecoach. In 1822, these merchants obtained a charter to build a canal from New Haven through Farmington to the Massachusetts border where it would connect with the Hampshire-Hampton canal to Northampton. Their aim was to have eventual access to the Saint Lawrence River. (As it turned out, the Farmington canal was open only a short while because it was plagued by many problems.)

Unwilling to be so bypassed, Hartford merchants joined together in the Connecticut River Company and secured a charter to promote navigation on the upper river. In 1826, the company built the *Barnet*, seventy-five feet long and fourteen and one half feet wide, but drawing only twenty-two inches of water, a size they thought would be able to pass through the locks beyond Enfield. She was named for the Vermont town she hopefully would be able to reach. (She never did.)

The *Barnet*'s first trip was to Bellows Falls, 125 miles north of Hartford. With a scow lashed to each side and thirty men poling her, she passed through the Enfield rapids. She was also able to pass through the South Hadley locks, and finally reached Bellows Falls. After celebrations all along the upper river, the *Barnet* returned to Hartford. In the words of the Boston *Daily Advertiser:*

> It ought not to be forgotten that this experiment was made under almost every disadvantage. The *Barnet* was built entirely since 22d August last . . . Yet success has followed the exertion, and when we look to future, we can see nothing to limit our hope that they who live on the fertile banks of the Connecticut, which are more thickly settled than those of any river of the same size in the Union, may soon be favored with all the advantages which come from the cheap, safe, regular, and quick communication afforded by steam navigation. There is nothing in the character of the river to set bounds to the course of improvement, short of the entire accomplishment of the object proposed.

Because of this success, Thomas Blanchard built several steamboats for the upper river, the *Blanchard* and the *Vermont*. The *Vermont* was eighty feet overall and drew just over a foot of water. On one of her trips to Bellows Falls, as she was passing through rapids below Brattleboro, the *Vermont*, in the words of Melancthon W. Jacobus,

> had come to a standstill, notwithstanding that the fire was so great that the blaze poured from the smokestack, and Capt. Blanchard, with the energy of despair, was pushing against the bed of the river with a spiked pole. To add to the excitement . . . . , Captain Blanchard fell overboard. Fortunately, he was caught by the coat collar and dragged out before he was swept under the keel.

Now that they had seen that small, specially built steamboats could navigate the upper river, the Hartford merchants proceeded to build a canal to bypass the Enfield rapids at what has since been named Windsor Locks. This was a major undertaking, for the canal was five and one half

The locks at Windsor Locks as they appear today.

miles long and seventy feet wide, with a series of three locks to accommodate steamboats and flatboats up to seventy-five tons. The canal opened in
1829, and from then on, regular service was possible between Hartford,
Springfield, and Holyoke.

Attempts at steamboat navigation beyond the Springfield, Vermont,
area did not meet with any success. The *Vermont*, which had been able to
pass through the Bellows Falls locks, was prevented by the width of her
beam from passing through the Hartland locks. In 1831, *John Ledyard*
was built, narrow enough to pass through the Hartland locks and with a
shallow draft to pass over sandbars. She got stuck on a sandbar at the
mouth of the Ammonoosuc River and never actually reached the town of
Wells River.

It was finally obvious that steamboats were uneconomical and im-
practical on this part of the river, so flatboats continued to be used to carry
on commerce with Hartford and the lower valley. Some of these were as
much as seventy-two feet in length and eleven feet in width, carrying
thirty tons of cargo but drawing only two or three feet of water. The boats
were rigged with a square sail which was supplemented with oars and
spike poles. Eight to ten flat boats made regular round trips to Hartford,
transporting lumber and farm products in exchange for manufactured
goods from the lower valley.

By 1836, Hartford had become an important transportation link on the
river, as described by Barber in his *Connecticut Historical Collections:*

> Hartford is very advantageously situated for business, is surrounded
> by an extensive and wealthy district, and communicates with the

112

towns and villages on the Connecticut above, by small steamboats, (now 8 in number) two of which, for passengers, ply daily between Hartford and Springfield. The remainder are employed in towing flat bottomed boats of 15 to 30 tons burthen, as far as Wells' river, 220 miles above the city. The coasting trade is very considerable, and there is some foreign trade, not extensive, carried on. Three steamboats form a daily line between here and New York.

Among the passengers from Springfield to Hartford in 1842 was Charles Dickens, and he recounted this journey in his *American Notes:*

... the winter having been unusually mild, the Connecticut River was 'open', in other words, not frozen. The captain of a small steam-boat was going to make his first trip for the season that day (the second February trip, I believe, within the memory of man) and only waited for us to go on board. Accordingly, we went on board, with as little delay as might be. He was as good as his word, and started directly.

It certainly was not called a small steam-boat without reason. I omitted to ask the question, but I should think it must have been of about half a pony power. Mr. Paap, the celebrated Dwarf, might have lived and died happily in the cabin, which was fitted with common sash-windows like an ordinary dwelling-house. These windows had bright red curtains, too, hung on slack strings across the lower panes; so that it looked like the parlour of a Lilliputian public-house, which had got

Harriet S. R. Eastman: *View of Hartford Waterfront.* About 1840.
Connecticut Historical Society.
Up river flatboats made many trips between Hartford and the upper river towns.

P. Fuerstenberg: *City of Hartford.* Wadsworth Atheneum.
   The *City of Hartford*, introduced in 1852, is shown in this painting at East Haddam. To the left is the East Haddam Ferry and on the right is the Gelston House. Of 970 tons and 273 feet long, she could carry 977 passengers along with 1,400 tons of cargo. Her interior was described in the *Courant:*

   "Her cabins and saloons are very spacious and elegantly fitted up with carpets of Brussells and velvet tapestry, in gorgeous patterns, curtains of satin brocatelle, rosewood chairs, sofas and settees, very easy and of beautiful and appropriate patterns, covered with the same material, rosewood tables and sideboards with marble tops, &c, &c, &c. On the upper deck are thirty-five staterooms of different sizes, some opening into others for the accommodation of families, all splendidly curtained and furnished — and two large 'Bridal Rooms,' in appearance rich enough to satisfy a Prince . . . ."

afloat in a flood or some other water accident, and was drifting nobody knew where. But even in this chamber there was a rocking-chair. It would be impossible to get anywhere, in America, without a rocking-chair.

I am afraid to tell how many feet short this vessel was, or how many feet narrow; to apply the words length and breadth to such measurement would be a contradiction in terms. But I can state that we all kept to the middle of the deck, lest the boat should unexpectedly tip over. The machinery, by some surprising process of condensation, worked between the deck and the keel, the whole forming a warm sandwich, about three feet thick.

It rained all day . . . The river was full of floating blocks of ice, which were constantly crunching and cracking under us; and the depth of water, in the course we took to avoid the larger masses, carried down the middle of the river by the current, did not exceed a few inches . . . .

After two hours and a half of this odd traveling (including a stoppage at a small town, where we were saluted by a gun considerably bigger than our own chimney), we reached Hartford . . .

   In spite of Dickens' tongue-in-cheek accounting of his steamboat ride to Hartford, these years on the lower river were highly successful for the steamboat. The lower half of the Connecticut River, Long Island Sound, Narragansett Bay, and the Hudson River were all full of steamers that furnished the best means of transportation in the days when the railroad was still in its infancy.

9

LATE VICTORIAN DAYS

On Monday, January 1, much to the astonishment of some, and gratification of all, the first train of cars ever seen in this vicinity passed over the Cheshire road and Sullivan [road] to Charlestown, New Hampshire. The day was fine and a great assembly of people had collected here to observe the grand entree of the Iron Horse. The engine came up in grand style and when opposite our village, the monster gave one of its most savage yells, frightening men, women, and children considerably, and bringing forth the most deafening howls from all the dogs in the neighborhood. This day, Thursday, the Sullivan road is to be opened, with the usual ceremonies, to Charlestown, and then the arrival of the cars will be a common, everyday business affair.

Bellows Falls Gazette
January 4, 1849

The railroad had arrived in the upper Connecticut River valley, where it was more than welcomed. Here, the river had never been very navigable, so travel by flatboat had been the only option. Thus, there was great jubilation when the railroad reached the area.

Railroad lines were quickly built all over the upper river valley, coming north from Springfield, west from Boston, and south from Montreal. By 1852, the greater part of the Vermont-New Hampshire reach was covered by railroads running along the river with branches into the interior towns. Some towns grew in importance because railroads converged on them from all directions. Woodsville, New Hampshire was one such town. It became a major railroad center with the attendant yards, an engine roundhouse, and other facilities. Tracks are still to be seen down the main street of town. White River Junction in Vermont was an important point on the lines from New York, and from Boston to Montreal. Springfield, Massachusetts also became an important railroad center, located as it was between Boston and Albany, and on the way to New York. With the completion of the railroad from New Haven through Hartford, Springfield, and northern cities, scheduled river transportation above Hartford came to an end.

In the lower river valley, the river remained as the principal artery of transportation between cities and towns. Steamboat interests feared they would lose their lucrative route between Hartford and New York, and they considered the railroad a major threat. To save the river from this competition, the steamboat interests began a fight against the railroads which was to continue for many years.

A railroad line had been completed from New York to New Haven in 1848, and on to New London several years later. However, the only way

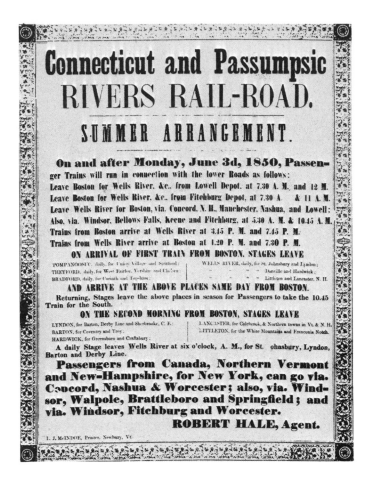

for the train to cross the Connecticut River at Old Saybrook was to ferry its passengers and freight across. A railroad bridge was the obvious solution, so the railroad interests petitioned the Connecticut Legislature for permission to build a bridge. They also wanted a railroad bridge for another rail line to cross at Middletown.

For the next twenty years, the steamboat interests used all their political power in the legislature to block these bills. A bill to permit a bridge between Old Lyme and Old Saybrook was defeated in 1866. A similar proposal for a bridge between Middletown and Portland was defeated the next year. Eventually, however, the legislature approved both bridges. The Middletown bridge opened in 1870 and the Old Lyme bridge a few years later. Also, in 1871, the Connecticut Valley Railroad was completed, running from Old Saybrook to Hartford. Now valley residents could travel from Hartford to New York, changing in Old Saybrook, thus considerably shortening their journey.

The steamboat companies, however, were tenacious and did not stop competing with the railroad, even though steamboats were to see their full share of problems in the years to come. Fires and accidents were just a few of their worries.

The Hartford and New York steamboat companies had merged and come out with the *City of Hartford* in 1852. In thirty-four years on the

The *City of Hartford* plowed into the Middletown railroad bridge on March 29, 1876 in a tremendous crash "heard all over the city." The pilot had confused a light on the shore with one on the bridge. The boat was salvaged and returned to the river under the name of *Capitol City*. Ten years later, in a dense fog and gale, the *Capitol City* piled up on the rocks near Rye Beach, New York, and was a total loss.

Artist Unknown: *City of Richmond*. Connecticut Historical Society.
  The *City of Richmond* is shown passing Cromwell in the 1880s, with the Valley Railroad in the background. The boat later caught fire at Peck's Slip in New York and was rebuilt, only to burn beyond repair off Greenwich in 1904.

Fenwick Hall, in Fenwick, south of Old Saybrook, was a large Victorian hotel
which represented the ultimate in resort hotel luxury. Families came by
steamboat from Hartford with all their summer paraphenalia, and men went
back and forth to Hartford on a daily basis on the newly opened Valley Railroad. Visitors without their own summer cottages could stay at Fenwick Hall.
The hotel burned down in 1917, long after its days of glory were gone.

river, she had two accidents, was totally refurbished, and finally crashed
on the rocks in a storm.

The *City of Hartford's* rival was Vanderbilt's *Granite State,* described in 1853 as "a trifle smaller than the *City of Hartford* but in every
respect worthy to be her associate in the navigation of the Connecticut.
On the upper deck is a long saloon beautfully carpeted and furnished with
settees, easy chairs . . . ." The *Granite State* was on the river for fourteen
years. On May 18, 1883, she met her end near Goodspeed's Landing in
East Haddam in a fire which began in the engine room. Captain Dibble
was able to run her up to the landing where some passengers clambered
ashore. Others were rescued by the East Haddam ferry and smaller river
craft. She was a total loss.

The costliest sidewheeler to serve on the river, and perhaps the least
lucky, was the *State of New York,* 281 feet long, 155 feet wide, and weigh-
ing 1,417 tons. She began her run in 1867. After hitting a rock on the Old
Saybrook breakwater in 1871, she piled up on a rock near Hell's Gate only
a few days later. In 1881, she caught fire and was beached near Goodspeed's Landing by Captain Dibble, who, two years later, was to beach
the *Granite State* at the same place. The *State of New York* was raised,
repaired, and returned to service as the *City of Springfield.* Further mis-
haps were to befall her on at least four occasions until, having been turned
into a coal barge, she eventually foundered in a storm off New Jersey.

Toward the end of the century, the steamboat company was in dire
financial trouble and was sold to creditors. Tenacity, however, won out
again. The company was reorganized, the ships were repurchased, and
their operations became more successful financially. New safety codes,
boiler inspections, improved navigational aids, and the substitution of
electricity for oil lights were effected to contribute to the new reliability of
steamboating.

Summer travel became increasingly popular. People were attracted
from Hartford and New York to the Goodspeed Opera House, the Gelston
House, or the Champion House in East Haddam; the Griswold Inn in
Essex; or the Pease House or Fenwick Hall at Saybrook Point.

In 1892, the company brought out the *Hartford,* the first propeller
steamer designed expressly for the Connecticut River run. Her speed was
fifteen knots, and she burned only half the coal consumed by the *City of
Springfield.* Upon the outbreak of the Spanish-American War in 1898, the
Hartford was purchased by the government for use as a military transport,
and she was replaced by a new *Hartford.* The *City of Springfield* had also
been replaced by the *Middletown.* The *Hartford* and the *Middletown*
were very similar, fairly close in tonnage, but the *Hartford* had two stacks.

The *Hartford* and the *Middletown* served for the next thirty-two sea-
sons of steamboat travel. Up to World War I, the service was good, safe,
and financially profitable. Trips were made with regularity, and schedules were strictly followed. The Hartford landing was at the foot of State

Standing on the east bank of the river is the Goodspeed Opera House, the tallest all-wood structure along the entire river. William H. Goodspeed, who
built the Opera House in 1876, owned an important shipyard in East Haddam
and was an enterpreneur of no mean talent.

After the Civil War, East Haddam became well known as a summer resort
with many visitors coming by boat from Hartford and New York. At that time,
the town had two river landings about a mile apart, owned by highly competi-
tive interests. The upper landing, also a ferry site, was near the Champion

House and the Maplewood Music Seminary where theater and music were offered to the public. The Goodspeed landing was the lower landing and was considered slightly less fashionable than the upper landing.

Goodspeed, being a dynamic and ambitious man, decided to establish his own hotel at the Gelston House, operate his own ferry across the river, and construct an opera house six stories high on the river bank. Construction began in 1876 and was completed within one year. There was a white and gold auditorium on the four upper floors, with red plush boxes in the balcony. The stage curtain depicted the *State of New York*, then the pride of Goodspeed's river fleet.

The first performance was reported in the Deep River *New Era* as follows:

"The weather on October 24, 1877, was very unfavorable to say the least; but in spite of that, about six hundred persons assembled in Goodspeed's new hall to witness the play and listen to the music as well as gaze on the beauties of that gem of an opera house. The first exclamation of every lady entering the hall was 'Splendid'! (with at least four notes of admiration) and that of the male bipeds was 'Gorgeous' with a similar apportionment of points; but neither adjective fits the case exactly. It is simply PERFECT, from the black walnut banister on the stairway to the ventilator, it is just perfect. The stage curtains and scenery, the floor, the seats, everything we would have had if we were going to build an opera house and Mr. Goodspeed was going to pay the bills. The principal play was the comedy of 'Charles II', followed by the farces 'Box and Cox', 'Turn Him Out'. The singing by the Madrigal Boys was heartily encored as was the musical monologue, 'The Blind Beggar', by Tom Whiffen. After the close of the performance a large company tripped the light fantastic to a late hour."

The steamboat line, the hospitality of the Gelston House, and the opera house riverfront bar brought customers from far and near to witness performances with the best New York casts Goodspeed could provide. Such celebrities as Minnie Maddern Fiske, Josh Billings, and Henry Ward Beecher were all at the Goodspeed at one time or another.

Goodspeed died in 1882, and his business operation went into a period of decline. The shipyard closed, and the ferry service terminated. Both the opera house and the steamboat line were taken over by the Hartford and New York Transportation Company, which was eventually absorbed by the New Haven Railroad. The East Haddam Bridge in 1913 took over the earlier location of the ferry. The bridge, with its 889-foot length, is one of the largest swing bridges in the world and permits the maintenance of two separate channels for river traffic.

The opera house fell upon evil days. In the 1930s, it was used as a warehouse for local merchants. In 1943, it was acquired by the state as a state highway garage. Nine years later, it was slated for demolition, but interested preservationists organized themselves as the Goodspeed Opera Foundation. They induced the legislature to sell the Foundation the building for the nominal sum of one dollar.

By 1963, the building was restored to its formal grandeur as one of the most beautiful summer theaters in the country. It has developed a national reputation as the home of the American musical comedy. Since 1963, more than 30 musicals have been revived, and more than twelve new ones have been introduced. Seven Goodspeed musicals have gone on to Broadway: "Man of La Mancha" in 1966, "Shenandoah" and "Very Good Eddie" in 1975, "Something's Afoot" and "Going Up" in 1976, "Annie" in 1977, and "Whoopee" in 1979.

It is curious to note that Marguerite Allis in her "Connecticut River," published in 1938 when Victoriana was at a low ebb, described the Goodspeed Opera as "The most extravagant, the most impossible of all monstrosities disfiguring the river shores . . ." and that the building had "remained to disfigure the landscape long after its usefulness had passed."

Street. Stops were made at Wethersfield, Glastonbury, South Glastonbury, Portland, Middletown, Middle Haddam, Haddam Neck and the two landings in East Haddam — Upper Landing and Goodspeed's. Then came Hadlyme, Chester, Deep River, Hamburg, the Steamboat Dock at Essex, Old Lyme and, finally, the sound was reached at Saybrook Point.

These prewar years of the *Hartford* and the *Middletown* were perhaps the best years of the river steamboats, but although the surface was calm, there were strong currents beneath. During these years, the New York, New Haven, and Hartford Railroad company undertook a program to monopolize all forms of transportation in southern New England — streetcars, urban lines, and steamer lines for freight and passengers. The company was so mismanaged that, in 1913, it did not have enough money to pay its dividend to shareholders. The quality of its services, both on rail and on ship, seriously declined. The river ships, which were to carry on for another eighteen years, became increasingly poorly managed. The landings along the river were equally neglected, and many became nothing more than rotted piers.

By 1930, the *Hartford* and the *Middletown* were aged, inefficient, and expensive to operate. The railroads had been responsible for their decline, but their actual demise now came about because of automobiles and new highways with readily available trucking facilities. Their doom was finally sealed in the great Depression following 1929. The last trip on the river was the Hartford's voyage on October 31, 1931.

The railroads were to meet some disasters of their own. A few miles north of White River Junction was the scene of one of the worst train wrecks in New England's history. On the night of February 5, 1887, the last four cars of the Montreal Express derailed while crossing a bridge over the White River. The cars, made of wood, fell from the bridge to the frozen river and were set on fire by the woodstoves used for heat. The bridge burned up also, and thirty-nine people were killed and forty-nine injured. The accident attracted nationwide attention and was one of the factors responsible for the enactment of the Railway Appliance Act of 1893, the first national legislation setting safety standards for railroad equipment.

Another disaster for the railroad was the competition it soon would receive from the automobile industry, and this began in the river valley. In Springfield, Massachusetts, the Duryea brothers built the first American, gas-propelled automobile in 1893. It was a two-horsepower gasoline engine attached to a ladies' phaeton. They won a fifty-mile race and used the prize money to build the first American automobile factory which, however, eventually succumbed to competition from Detroit.

Farmers also felt the effect of the railroad. Railroads brought midwestern crops to the important markets along the eastern seaboard. Vermont and New Hampshire Merino sheepraisers now faced competition from the west which had vast grazing areas. Their sheep were no longer economically viable. The farmers then decided to use the railroad to their advantage and turned their efforts to dairy products, fruits, vegetables, and poultry which could be readily shipped by rail to the Boston and New York markets.

Emigration from New England to the west and midwest continued, now via the railroad, as people sought more wide open spaces. The effect

The Victorian-style Essex Steamboat Dock (now the River Museum), shown in this birds-eye print at the foot of Main Street, was built in 1879. Birdseye prints were exceedingly popular in the 1880s. The Essex print was published by Bailey and Company of Boston, who made similar prints of many New England towns. Also shown in the print is the long rope walk, left center, running parallel with Main Street. There are five churches on the hill including, at the far right, the Baptist Church (1845) which is an interesting example of Egyptian Revival architecture, very much akin to the well-known example at Sag Harbor, Long Island.

of emigration was offset by the arrival of new groups of people into all parts of the river valley. Here again the railroad was involved. The Irish were the first to come, being brought in to help build canals and railroads. The Irish were followed by Germans, and later in the century by Scandinavians, Italians, Poles, and Slavs. These were the years when over 600 stonecutters came to America, most of them from Italy, to live and work at new quarries on Selden's Neck, Joshua's Rock, and Brockway's Landing across the river from the town of Deep River. A large influx of French-Canadians came in as workers to the milltowns of Holyoke and Springfield, and to the smaller towns of Vermont and New Hampshire.

By 1870, the foreign-born totaled 113,639 and constituted thirty-one percent of the population of Connecticut. In Holyoke alone, between 1855 and 1895, the population of 4,600 increased tenfold.

The once homogeneous population of the river valley was gone. The arrival of people from all over the world who spoke a different language and had very different religious and social traditions from those of the old Yankees caused many problems at first. In the course of time, however, these new people were assimilated into the river valley civilization.

Despite the newcomers, however, the old Yankees remained firmly in the saddle. They were in complete control of industry, banks, shipping interests, and railroads, to say nothing of the political scene which they had dominated through the century. The Republican party carried on in the old Federalist tradition, and the Democratic party was almost as conservative. The legislatures were generally weighted in favor of small rural communities, thus giving them a wholly disproportionate control over the political process. This situation was to continue for another sixty or so years, until the Supreme Court, in 1965, handed down its "one man, one vote" decision which was to lead to legislative reapportionment through a good part of the country.

The face of the cities changed considerably during these years, as communities grew in prosperity as well as size. Hartford was boastful of its new Victorian Gothic State Capitol building built in 1880 and its broad parks designed by Horace Bushnell. Springfield was becoming the metropolis of western Massachusetts. Chicopee's City Hall, with a 147-foot tower modeled on that of the Palazzo Vecchio in Florence, Italy, was built in 1870. In Northampton, where the City Hall had been built in 1848, the

Until 1875, Connecticut had two state capitols, alternating between Hartford and New Haven every other year. Eventually Hartford won out, and in 1879 a new state capitol, designed by Richard M. Upjohn, was completed. The Victorian Gothic structure on the hill in Bushnell Park is a departure from the traditional neoclassical style typical of most American state capitols. It has been highly praised — "exuberant and eclectic in spirit" (*Connecticut Guide*, 1938), and roundly condemned — ."the most ridiculous building I know of" (Frank Lloyd Wright).

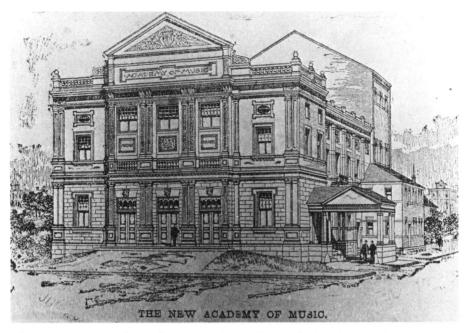

THE NEW ACADEMY OF MUSIC.

The Northampton Academy of Music was the focal point of cultural and intellectual life in Northampton during the prosperous latter half of the nineteenth century. Northampton also developed into a popular resort as a watering spa.

In the eighteenth and nineteenth centuries, two of the most learned families in the nation, the Dwights and the Whitneys, who were interrelated, came from Northampton. Timothy Dwight, a grandson of Jonathan Edwards, was President of Yale, a confirmed Federalist, author, poet, and theologian, and deeply attached to his native Connecticut River valley. His brother, Theodore, was famous for his political pamphlets and satires, and served as secretary of the Hartford Convention of 1815. His grandson, Timothy, also served as president of Yale from 1886 to 1898.

Josiah Dwight Whitney with his two wives produced thriteen children, of whom nine lived to maturity. There was a son, Josiah Dwight Whitney, eminent geologist, whose name adorns Mt. Whitney in Alaska; William Dwight Whitney, philologist and eminent Sanskrit scholar; Maria Whitney, professor of modern languages at Smith College; and James Lyman Whitney, the distinguished librarian of the Boston Public Library.

Memorial Hall was built in 1871 and the Academy of Music in 1891. Sarah Bernhardt, Maude Adams, and Ellen Terry made appearances at the Academy in later years. In St. Johnsbury, Vermont, a large town on the Passumpsic River which is a tributary of the Connecticut, descendants of Thaddeus Fairbanks, the inventor of the first level scale and founder of the Fairbanks Morse Scale Works, were responsible for two buildings, an art gallery, and a museum.

The Atheneum Art Gallery was given to St. Johnsbury in 1871 by Horace Fairbanks, who later became governor of Vermont. Fairbanks also gave his magnificent art collection of sixteenth and seventeenth century European paintings and sculptures and his nineteenth century paintings of the so-called Hudson River School. One painting is Albert Bierstadt's enormous "The Domes of the Yosemite," painted in 1867, and described in the *New York Times* of the day as being "worth a week's travel to see."

The Museum of Natural Science, given by Franklin Fairbanks in 1891, is a fine architectural work in the Richardson Romanesque style. It has collections of birds, mammals, reptiles, fish, minerals, flora, and extensive agricultural implements.

In cities as well as in smaller towns, successful merchants, businessmen, writers, and artists built beautiful homes, many of them large, rambling, Victorian houses, where they lived in a certain luxury and a degree of contentment which came from achievement.

Samuel Clemens, better known as Mark Twain, built a home in Hartford during these years. In 1868, he had first visited Hartford and had written, "Of all the beautiful towns it has been my fortune to see, this is the chief." Five years later, Clemens and his wife moved to Hartford because it was then an important publishing center where many literary people lived. He commissioned Edward Tuckerman Potter to design a house. The result was a huge, rambling, red and yellow, Victorian Gothic structure on Farmington Avenue. The first floor was decorated by Louis C. Tiffany. As described in *The Hartford Courant,* "The novelty displayed in the architecture of the building, the oddity of its internal arrangements, and the fame of its owner will all conspire to make it a house of note for a long time to come."

In the rear of the house, an addition was constructed in the form of a pilothouse as a reminder of Clemens' days as a Mississippi River pilot.

Twain wrote about the house, "To us, our house was not unsentient matter — it had a heart and a soul . . . It was of us, and we were in its

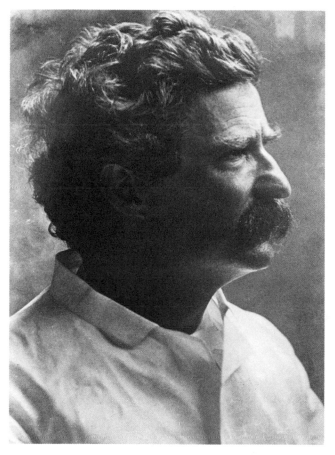

Mark Twain lived in Hartford from 1871 to 1896. Among his works written in Hartford were: *Tom Sawyer, Huckleberry Finn, Life on the Mississippi, The Prince and the Pauper,* and *A Connecticut Yankee in King Arthur's Court.* The Twains were well-known hosts. Some of the leading figures of the day who, at one time or another, dined at Twain's Hartford house included William Dean Howells, General William T. Sherman, General Philip H. Sheridan, Edwin Booth, Sir Henry Stanley, Rudyard Kipling, Bret Harte, Thomas B. Aldrich, and Thomas Nast. Twain was a great epicure. His seventieth birthday dinner at Delmonico's in New York featured fillet of kingfish, saddle of lamb, Baltimore tarpon, and quail among other victuals.

confidence, and lived in its grade and in the peace of its benediction. We never came home from an absence that its face did not light up and speak out its eloquent welcome — and we could not enter it unmoved."

Adjacent to the Twain home is the Harriet Beecher Stowe house, a mid-Victorian "cottage" where the author of *Uncle Tom's Cabin* lived from 1873 until her death in 1896. Both houses are now part of the Nook Farm Complex which also includes a research library covering not only the writers and intellectuals who lived at Nook Farm, but also the related social history, literature, arts, and architecture of the late nineteenth century.

Mark Twain's Hartford house on Farmington Avenue about 1880.

Twain's Hartford period ended in tragedy. Due to financial reverses, his house was closed in 1891, and Twain went on a world lecture tour to raise funds to pay his debts. On the way home from England in 1896, his eldest daughter died of spinal meningitis. Because of the tragedy, the family never returned to Hartford to live. The house was sold in 1903. Falling upon evil days, the house was almost destroyed, but it was eventually saved and fully restored as the Mark Twain Memorial in 1974.

Other prominent authors who were intimately connected with Hartford were Edmund C. Stedman and Charles Dudley Warner. Important artists from Hartford included Thomas Cole, Frederick E. Church, Charles Noel Flagg, and Dwight Tryon. The historian, John Fiske; Horace Bushnell, the theologian and pioneer in the development of Hartford's parks; and Henry Barnard, educator and colleague of Horace Mann, all lived in Hartford during these years.

The writer, Edward Bellamy, made his home in Chicopee, Massachusetts, at this time. Bellamy was the author of *Looking Backward*, one of the most popular American utopian romances of the time.

Poet Emily Dickinson was another important river valley woman of the time, though it has only been in recent years that she has been recognized as one of the great poets in American literature. She lived almost her entire life as a recluse in Amherst. Only seven of her poems were published in her lifetime, but over 1,000 were discovered by her sister after her death. Many more were found in old boxes in the attic by a subsequent owner of the Dickinson house.

In Springfield, Massachusetts, Samuel Bowles was one of the foremost American newspaper editors. He made the *Springfield Republican*, founded by his father in 1824, into one of the half dozen most influential papers in the United States. Bowles was also a close friend of the family of Emily Dickinson in Amherst and did much to encourage her writing of poetry.

In Cornish, New Hampshire, Augustus Saint-Gaudens, one of America's foremost sculptors, built a home with a studio and beautiful gardens, which has since become a National Historic Site. Saint-Gaudens was the sculptor of the statue of Lincoln in Chicago, the Puritan in Springfield, the Shaw Memorial in Boston, the memorial to Mrs. Henry Adams in Wash-

The Saint-Gaudens National Historic Site in Cornish, New Hampshire, contains the home, studio, and gardens of Augustus Saint-Gaudens (1848-1907).

Henry James (1843-1916) lived in Northampton on Round Hill Road overlooking the Connecticut River in the latter part of 1864. Here he wrote articles and reviews for the *North American Review*. He chose Northampton for the setting of the beginning of his first novel, *Roderick Hudson*. When James returned to Northampton in 1905 for a lecture at Smith College, he posed for a series of photographs by Katherine Elizabeth McClellan, a Smith graduate of 1882. These remarkable photos are to be seen in the William Allan Neilson Library at the college.

ington's Rock Creek cemetery, and the monument to General Sherman in front of New York's Plaza Hotel.

The importance of education continued to be stressed throughout the river valley. Dwight Lyman Moody, a great American evangelist, founded the Northfield Seminary for girls in 1879 and the Mount Hermon School for boys three years later. Almost one hundred years later, these schools were merged into the Northfield-Mount Hermon School. Smith College was founded in 1871 in Northampton. This was made possible through a bequest of Sophia Smith for the founding of a women's college "not to render my sex any the less feminine, but to develop as fully as may be the powers of womanhood."

The five daughters of Zephaniah Smith, who lived in a house dating from 1740 in Glastonbury, were rather unusual women for their time. Their names were as remarkable as their talents: Nancy Zephina, a mechanical genius; Cyrinthia Sacretia; Laurilla Aleroyla, an artist; Julia Evelina, a scholar who made five translations of the Bible, one from Latin, two from Greek and two from Hebrew; and Abby Hadassah. The last two sisters were militant abolitionists and early suffragettes. They refused to pay town taxes on the grounds that they were denied the right to vote, with the consequence that, on several occasions, their cows were seized and put up for auction. Their friends successfully bid on the cows and returned them to the sisters. Much publicity was given to their case. They were strongly supported by the respected Samuel Bowles of the *Springfield Republican* who wrote:

> Is taxation without representation, which was wrong in Boston in 1774, right in Glastonbury in 1874? That is the issue forced upon the intelligent, justice-loving people of Connecticut .... by these women.

In 1877, Abby died, leaving Julia, then eighty-five, alone on the farm. Not to be nonplussed, five years later, she married a widower of eighty-five and lived happily for eight more years.

The end of the century saw the culmination of great changes in the river valley. While in 1800 Dartmouth was the only collegiate institution in the valley, by 1900 Wesleyan, Trinity, Smith, Mount Holyoke, and Amherst were all well-established colleges with national reputations for excellence. Fine museums and public buildings had been established. Many writers and artists had discovered the area, and more were to come. Numerous industries were clustered in the valley, with an effect on the river that was very shortly to be felt. Agriculture had become relatively unimportant, and many farms had been deserted. The days of shipbuilding were over, fishing was no longer a booming commercial venture, and the discovery of cement had finished the quarrying days. The river was no longer the main artery of transportation, and it had lost its earlier role as the unifying factor of the valley. The middle class had spread out from the centers of the cities to newly built homes in the residential areas that were being opened. The lowest groups on the economic ladder were obviously the least well off, but they fared better in the river valley than did their counterparts in the ghettos of New York and Boston.

This, then, was the Connecticut River valley as it moved into the twentieth century.

Janet Cummings Good: *Rudyard Kipling*, from a drawing by William Strang in the National Portrait Gallery (London)

With a beautiful setting overlooking the river, Brattleboro, Vermont, attracted numerous writers and artists in the late nineteenth century, the best known of whom was Rudyard Kipling. Kipling's wife was a Brattleboro girl, and they lived near her family from 1892 to 1896. Although Kipling wrote *Captains Courageous*, *Just So Stories*, and the *Jungle Books* during these years, his stay in Brattleboro was not a happy one. The local people resented Mrs. Kipling's affectations and Rudyard's aloofness which almost amounted to scorn and disdain. Kipling thought his brother-in-law irresponsible and prone to excessive drinking. There was friction and quarreling between them until Kipling brought legal charges against the brother for threats. The brother was arrested on a criminal complaint, and the Kiplings became the laughing stock of Brattleboro. It was not long before the Kiplings left for England, never to return. Kipling is reported to have said, "There are only two places in the world where I want to live — Bombay and Brattleboro. And I can't live in either."

10

PROGRESS AND NEGLECT

Be it known to all persons that I, Nathaniel Matson Terry, of the Town of Old Lyme, County of New London, State of Connecticut, being over ninety years of age and still sound of mind and body, this condition being due in part to strict attention to regular work and lifelong interest and participation in out-of-door sports, so that as far back as I can remember I recall hardly a day that I was not well enough to ride on horseback or sail a boat; but well knowing that sometime, and I hope not very soon, there must be an end to my life on earth, I do revoke any and all former wills and do make, publish and declare this as my Last Will and Testament . . .

Nathaniel Matson Terry
Old Lyme, 1938

The Connecticut River valley people were hearty folk, and Terry was no exception. They always derived simple enjoyment from the river — swimming, fishing, boating, and appreciating nature. The people took these pleasures for granted, because they had always been available. It was during the first half of the twentieth century, however, that these simple pleasures were almost lost forever due to man's neglect and abuse of the river.

Little thought had ever been given to the use of the river as a dumping ground for industrial wastes and sewage from towns bordering its banks. Now, however, because of the population and industry growth of the late nineteenth century, the river was being increasingly polluted. Swimming in the river, which in years gone by had been the delight of country youngsters, became a health hazard. The shad catch, which had once exceeded 28,000 a day, was reduced to a total of half that number for the entire season in 1922. The salmon had long since disappeared, and the bird population in the marshes along the river had greatly diminished.

There was little general interest in the environmental or aesthetic impact the dams, factories, and mills had on the river. By 1930, the river had been dammed in fourteen spots — one in Connecticut at Enfield, two in Massachusetts at Holyoke and Turner's Falls, and eleven along the Vermont-New Hampshire border. New factories and mills were built along the riverfront, few of them with the architectural merit of the fine brick mills of the mid-nineteenth century. Many of these new buildings served their purpose and then rapidly fell into disuse due, in no small degree, to the competition from other parts of the country. With this deterioration came the rubbish dumps, the junk piles, and a general disfiguration of the riverbanks. Hartford, Windsor Locks, Enfield, Springfield, Chicopee, Holyoke, Brattleboro, Bellows Falls, and Windsor, Vermont, suffered, and even now, the fruits of this neglect are all too apparent. Even in rural areas, the river became isolated and inaccessible, being hedged in by jungles of weeds, bushes and trees.

What man was doing to the river environment through his abuse and neglect was in a way equaled by nature itself. There had been heavy floods in 1854, 1862, 1866, 1909, and 1913, but during the second quarter of the century, a series of floods and hurricanes brought to the area disasters unparalleled in modern times. The devastation was due in no small degree to the wreckless abandon with which the river valley had been

The Windsor-Cornish bridge over the Connecticut River, built in 1866, was sturdy enough to survive the flood of 1936 and the hurricane of 1938. The bridge is 460 feet long, the longest covered bridge in America. The first bridge in this location was built in 1796 and was rebuilt three times until it was swept away in the flood of 1865.

The second longest covered bridge in the country until its destruction in 1979, was the Bedell Bridge, with a length of 396 feet. This was the fifth bridge built over the river between South Newbury and Haverhill. The first bridge was built in 1805, was damaged by a flood and rebuilt in 1823, only to be swept away eighteen years later. A third bridge was carried away by a spring flood in 1862. The fourth was destroyed in a storm on the 4th of July in 1866. The fifth bridge, built the same year, was in active use until it was closed to traffic in 1968 because of its deteriorating condition. Various attempts to restore the bridge were made, but before it could be restored, it was almost destroyed in the spring and summer floods of 1973.

The bridge was about to be abolished in October of that year, but vigorous community protests resulted in the formation of a "Save the Bedell Bridge Committee." Over $250,000 was raised from various sources for its reconstruction. By 1978, the bridge had been rebuilt, and a state park was created around it. The restored bridge and the state park were dedicated in an elaborate celebration on July 22, 1979, with church services, parades, and flotillas of canoes.

Nature again took its toll, however, and on September 14, 1979, the restored bridge was completely destroyed by a windstorm in the wake of a hurricane. Thus came to an end the history of the Bedell Bridge at Haverhill, now only a part of history memorialized by the state park bearing its name.

Today, other covered bridges over the river are at Lancaster-Lunenberg, Columbia-Lemington, and Pittsburg-Clarkville. In addition, there are almost one hundred covered bridges in Vermont, more than all of the other New England states together.

despoiled of its natural resources in trees, shrubbery, and marshlands which had previously absorbed the rising waters of the river after severe rainstorms.

In 1927, severe floods occurred in the upper valley of the Connecticut, caused by a heavy November rainfall over frozen ground. The worst damage was in Vermont and New Hampshire where roads, railroad beds, and bridges were badly hit. The cost of the devastation exceeded fifteen million dollars, and some twenty people were killed.

Even more damage was caused by the flood of March, 1936, which set all the records for water destruction in the valley. The months of January and February had been unusually cold, and there was considerable snow throughout New England. In early March, a quick thaw, accompanied by torrential rains, resulted in vast amounts of water flowing from all over the valley in Vermont and New Hampshire down to the lower valley. By the twelfth of March, the river was twenty-eight point seven feet higher than normal in Springfield, and by the twentieth of the month the river rose to thirty-seven point six feet in Hartford. Eleven lives were lost; roads became impassable; fuel, electricity, and telephones were cut off for days. The total damage exceeded one hundred million dollars, with the bulk of the damage occurring in Massachusetts and Connecticut.

As a result of the flood, a series of dikes were built along the riverbanks from Northampton down through Hartford to contain the river. These were put to the test when the great hurricane of 1938 crossed the sound after striking Long Island and blew up the lower river valley. Thousands of homes and factories were destroyed; boats in the river were sunk or driven ashore; communities were flooded; and many of the great maples and elms which had graced the principal thoroughfares for years were uprooted. In Hartford, the waters reached thirty-five feet and threatened to loosen another great flood, but the dikes and embankments held fast. The water was also contained with sand bags placed at critical spots by a large army of volunteers. Even so, the damage of the hurricane in Connecticut alone reached over one hundred million dollars, with a toll of eighty-five dead.

The dikes and embankments would prove their value again during the hurricanes of 1954 and 1955, but they blocked the view of the river from the streets. The view also was marred by the railroad tracks, and later by the highways, that were built along the riverfront of many large towns, thus effectively cutting off these communities from the enjoyment of their historic river heritage.

The age of the automobile arrived, bringing with it the decline of the railroad, just as the railroad had brought the decline of the steamboat. Passengers now chose to travel by automobile on the new highways built to accommodate the ever-increasing traffic. All railroad passenger service from Hartford to Old Saybrook ended in 1934, but some service continued along the upper river in Vermont and New Hampshire until 1965. Thereafter, except for the through lines from New York to Hartford, Springfield, Boston, and Montreal, all passenger service disappeared from the river valley. Even the through lines had their time of travail with the 1970 bankruptcy of the Penn-Central system, which had taken over the New Haven lines some years before. Eventually, however, they were rescued through the establishment of the Amtrak network.

The *Hartford*, the last of the Connecticut River steamboats, left Hartford for
New York on October 31, 1931, never to return.

Trucks took over much of the freight traffic of the railroads, though a
few freight trains have lingered on. Bulk cargoes going to the industries
around Hartford continued to be carried by barges and oil tankers on the
river, which by this time constituted its only commercial traffic.

The rise and fall of the railroad was mirrored by other occurrences
along the river during these years. This was a time of many highs and
lows, prosperity and depression, war and peace.

In the first quarter of the century, the Connecticut River valley experienced growth and prosperity, particularly in the commercial and manufacturing areas around Hartford and Springfield. This growth was spurred
by increased immigration, so that by 1910, the foreign-born constituted
almost one-third of the Connecticut population of 1,114,756. By 1930,
sixty-five percent of the population of Massachusetts were either foreign-
born or of foreign and mixed parentage. Growth was practically static in
New Hampshire and Vermont where rural conditions continued to
prevail.

This prosperity continued through the years of World War I, when
valley industries were called upon to produce large amounts of munitions, clothing, and other articles for the military forces. In Hartford, Colt
Firearms produced its .45 service pistol along with newly designed machine guns and automatic rifles. The Springfield Arsenal turned out over
one quarter of a million 1903 Springfield rifles, as well as machine guns.
Scattered throughout the valley were large numbers of small plants all
making their contributions to the war effort.

The growth and prosperity of the first quarter of the century also came
about because many river valley towns were being discovered by an increasing number of artists and renowned people. Maxfield Parrish, perhaps America's best known commercial artist and illustrator, whose works
were widely reproduced on book and magazine covers such as the *Satur-*

day Evening Post, Collier's, the *Ladies' Home Journal,* and *Harpers,* lived near Cornish, New Hampshire. His home and studio, which overlook the Connecticut River, have been turned into a museum.

The American novelist, Winston Churchill, had a summer home in Cornish, known as Harlakenden House. The house served as Woodrow Wilson's summer White House in 1913, 1914, and 1915. Presidents in those days had a less hectic life than today's presidents, and Wilson was able to stay about six weeks during the summer of 1915. It was during this stay that he became engaged to Mrs. Edith Galt, who became his second wife in December of that year. (The marriage was not generally well received, as the first Mrs. Wilson had died only the year before. Politicians feared that Wilson's early remarriage might have adverse repercussions in the election of 1916.)

Other notables spending their summers in Cornish in these years included Herbert D. Croly, famed editor of the *New Republic;* Norman Hapgood, the journalist; and Percy MacKaye, the poet.

In Old Lyme, Connecticut, an artist colony of leading American impressionists of the day thrived. The themes of American impressionism revolved around the simple bucolic life of the countryside, the shoreline, and the sea. All of these were to be found in Old Lyme with its tree-lined streets, beautiful homes, and shoreline and salt meadows along the river and sound. The haven of the group was the William Noyes House, now better known as the Florence Griswold House, a graceful Greek Revival house designed and built by Samuel Belcher in 1817.

The house had been inherited by Florence Griswold from her sea captain father, Robert Griswold. Having come upon difficult times in 1899, she began to take in young artists as summer boarders. Among those who stayed at the house were Childe Hassam, Willard Metcalf, Allen Talcott, William Chadwick, Arthur Heming, Walter Griffin, Harry L. Hoffman, William H. Foote, Henry C. White, and Louis P. Dessar.

As an expression of appreciation for the hostess, the artists made paintings on various doors on the first floor, on fireplace mantelpieces, and on dining room panels.

Woodrow Wilson and his family were frequent guests at the Griswold House in the days of his Princeton presidency and, as he wrote to Arthur Heming some years later, the "memory of those carefree days in Lyme is still very fresh with me and very fragrant." In his memoirs "Miss Florence and the Artists of Old Lyme," Arthur Heming recounts that on one occasion when the Wilson family arrived, the ladies were seated at one table and that "Dr. Wilson was, of course, given a seat at the men's table, and it wasn't long before we not only realized his interest in art, literature and music, but we discovered that he was an excellent storyteller. So good indeed that I have long regretted that I did not keep a record of them. And in looking back over the years, I remember him as a combination of firmness and tolerance, intellect and godliness; a man of affairs, yet a scholar, a thinker, yet a doer. And I thoroughly enjoyed his friendship. At first Dr. Wilson seemed out of place at the men's table when he wore his coat. Three days later, however, he discarded it, though he never did unbend enough to roll up his shirt sleeves."

Ray Stannard Baker in his Pulitzer Prize-winning biography of Wilson tells us that "He loved particularly the town and quiet countryside

Childe Hassam: *Church at Old Lyme.* 1924. Lyme Historical Society.

Of unusual beauty is the Old Lyme town green with its superb white-spired Congregational Church and its surrounding houses where Washington and LaFayette were entertained in the Revolutionary War days, and to which La-Fayette returned on his trip through the United States in 1824. The church was considered to be one of the most perfect of the early nineteenth-century churches in New England. It has been the subject of many paintings by well-known artists, including Childe Hassam, who painted it three times in addition to this etching. The original church, designed by Samuel Belcher in 1817, burned in 1907. It was copied as closely as possible in the new structure which was dedicated in 1910. The principal address at the dedication was given by Woodrow Wilson, then president of Princeton University, and a frequent summer visitor of Old Lyme. Wilson had known the Connecticut River Valley since his Wesleyan days in Middletown where he was professor of history and political economy from 1888 to 1890.

135

of Old Lyme in Connecticut. Here were stately trees to shade the broad roads, and homes that bore themselves with the dignity of gracious living. An artist colony, sensitive to the charms of New England at its best, had long made the town a place of summer retirement . . . he returned year after year, finally expressing his attachment by considering the purchase of a permanent summer home."

The Florence Griswold House was designed in 1817 by Samuel Belcher for William Noyes and turned into a summer colony for American Impressionist artists by Florence Griswold. Upon Miss Florence's death in 1937, the *New York Times* editorialized her as follows:

"Florence Griswold was born on Christmas Day. The next would have been her eighty-seventh. She came into the news and into the hearts of many of us last year when the artists to whom she had been so kind in their hard-up days associated themselves to buy her house, mortgaged to the ridgepole, give her a home for life and then make it a public, as it has long been a private, museum. Their project was defeated, but by courtesy of the higher bidder, she was permitted to die in the house where she was born . . . .

"In her delicate and high-bred way, Miss Florence had her part in fostering an authentic American art. Fortunately, her painters painted her again and again, and many a down-at-heel artist left on her walls panels on other subjects signed by names that were to become distinguished. So the memory of this gracious and generous spirit survives, and not in Griswold House alone but as part of no inconsiderable chapter in the history of our native art."

Today the Florence Griswold house is owned by the Lyme Historical Society and is open to the public. Adjacent to it is the gallery of the Lyme Art Association, erected and financed in 1922 by many of the artists of the Old Lyme Group on land donated by Miss Griswold.

A rather unusual home — a castle — was built on the river during these years of prosperity by another notable person.

Best known for his role as Sherlock Holmes in the dramatization of Arthur Conan Doyle's work, and also the author of some twenty plays of his own, William Gillette was a huge success on the stage. He had amassed a considerable personal fortune. Born of a distinguished Hartford family and a direct descendant of Thomas Hooker, Gillette knew and loved the Connecticut River. In search of a place to build a home in 1913, Gillette was cruising the river and anchored his 140-foot houseboat just above the Chester-Hadlyme Ferry. Struck by the scenic beauty of the river at that point, he forthwith decided to build on the site. Fortunately he was able to purchase over one hundred acres. In 1914, he undertook the construction of a new home inspired, it was said, by the Normandy fortress of Robert LeDiable, father of William the Conqueror. Gillette's Castle was completed in 1919, and Gillette lived there until he died in 1937.

William Gillette's castle was completed in 1919. Gillette not only designed the castle with its granite walls four-to-five-feet thick and its twenty-four odd-shaped rooms, but also each door with its intricate locks, the light fixtures and most of the furniture. A railroad buff, Gillette also designed and built a railroad to transport the workers and materials to the site. This was later to serve as a miniature railroad carrying guests around the castle grounds and down to the river over a three-mile course.

Gillette enjoyed his castle for almost twenty years, dying in 1937 at the age of eighty-seven. He specified in his will that the property should not "fall into the hands of some blithering saphead who had no conception of where he is or with what surrounded." The property was on the market for a number of years. Finally, in 1943 it was acquired by the state, and it is now one of the most popular state parks in Connecticut with over 125 acres, beautiful hiking trails, and picnic facilities.

After graduating from Amherst, Calvin Coolidge moved to Northampton in 1897 where he practiced law until he became Mayor in 1910. In 1929, after he chose "not to run" for a further presidential term, Coolidge returned to his simple two-family house at 21 Massoit Street, amidst some comment that the dwelling was hardly suitable for an ex-president. This probably did not bother Coolidge as much as the lack of privacy, and a year later he purchased the "Beeches," a nine-acre estate with a 12-room house, swimming pool, and tennis court. As to what use he made of the last two items, we have no record. Named for the president, the Calvin Coolidge Memorial Bridge across the river to Hadley replaced an earlier one destroyed in the 1936 flood.

After World War I, the valley, like the rest of the country, experienced a post-war depression in 1920. This was followed by a short-lived prosperity under the administration of Calvin Coolidge, culminating in the bubble which burst in 1929, leaving in its wake the great Depression of the 1930s.

For New England as a whole, the Depression years were exceedingly difficult ones. The important textile and leather industries suffered steep declines. Factories were closed and unemployment increased. Eastern New Hampshire, the Boston area, and Rhode Island were the hardest hit. The river valley towns, on the other hand, were not quite as adversely affected by the Depression. Their industries were very diversified in nature, and much of the population was employed by the relatively stable insurance industry in Hartford and Springfield. The small towns along the river did not suffer from the widespread unemployment of the metropolitan areas. In fact, their economies were somewhat enriched by the beginnings of automobile tourism and the increasing attraction of the river valley as a vacation spot.

One of the many vacationers was Albert Einstein, who visited Old Lyme in 1935. Einstein, having sailed on a small inland lake near Berlin, decided to rent a Cape Cod Knockabout to sail on the river. Unfamiliar with the intricate currents and the sandbars and tides, he was said to have spent more time aground than afloat. The *New London Day* wrote about his adventure with the headline, "Einstein's Miscalculation Leaves Him Stuck on Bar of Lower Connecticut River."

World War II, which followed soon thereafter, had a considerable impact upon the life of the river valley. Thousands of men joined the armed forces, either as volunteers or through the draft. The river valley, with its tremendous production facilities, was swamped with defense contracts, and factories worked around the clock with three working shifts. Foremost in importance was the production of aircraft in the Hartford — Springfield — Middletown areas, followed by ordnance supplies, particularly rifles, machine guns, and munitions.

The years after the war saw a phenomenal expansion of the economy throughout the country, and the river valley industries shared in the general prosperity.

Springfield, now the third largest city in Massachusetts, has an unusually large number of public buildings, most of which are located in close proximity to each other in the revitalized and attractive downtown area. The so-called Quadrangle has four excellent museums: The George Walter Vincent Smith Art Museum, with one of the finest collections of Japanese arts and armour outside the Orient; the Springfield Museum of Science, with the Seymour Planetarium; the Connecticut Valley Historical Museum; and the Museum of Fine Arts with nineteen galleries of European and American painting and sculpture (including Erastus Field's famous Historical Monument of the American Republic), and Chinese bronzes and ceramics. (Museums are shown from right to left.) Close to the riverbank is the "Municipal Group" with the neoclassical city hall on one side and Symphony Hall on the other, with the 300-foot Florentine Campanile in the middle.

While a few industries, particularly textiles, eventually moved out of the river valley, most of the old, established industries prospered and expanded. These were hardware industries in Middletown; aircraft components, electrical equipment and insurance around Hartford; printing and paper products, rubber and sporting goods in the Springfield — Chicopee — Holyoke area; and machine tools around Springfield and Windsor, Vermont.

In addition, new industries now were attracted to the river towns. One attraction was the excellent labor force with high mechanical skills. Such industries as electronics, computers, precision instruments, light metal works, plastics, and sophisticated hardware moved into the valley and today represent a large proportion of its industrial output.

Air transport now served the area, which facilitated transportation of industrial products. Bradley Airport came into being for the Hartford-Springfield area, and innumerable small airports are to be found up and down the river from Chester, Connecticut, to Colebrook, New Hampshire.

New highways also were constructed, but happily, their impact on the countryside was taken into consideration.

An interstate highway program of the 1960s brought about the construction of I–91, running up the valley through Cromwell, Hartford, and Springfield; along the river to St. Johnsbury, Vermont; and then on to the Canadian border. A more scenic road, at least in the Vermont sector, would be hard to envisage. Equally striking south of Middletown is the Chester Bowles Highway leading to the mouth of the river at Old Saybrook. With these new highways came new bridges at Glastonbury, Hartford, Windsor, and Springfield.

Vermont and New Hampshire now became more accessible. Resorts which had been limited to the summer trade were now opened on a year-round basis as ski centers. The attractions of Vermont and New Hampshire for vacation or retirement living resulted in an escalation of land prices through new developments. The situation became particularly acute in Vermont where remaining farmers were being driven off their lands by the high taxes based on current assessed values. Act 250 passed by the Vermont Legislature in 1970 brought in some measure of control by laying down stringent conditions for the approval of new developments.

Vermont farmers learned to turn the super-highways to their advantage. They began to supply most of the dairy products of Boston and New York. Dairy products are still produced in abudance today, as are apples, corn, and maple sugar, and the highways provide a ready access to urban markets. Logging is the principal activity in northern Vermont and New Hampshire, where trees and wood products constitute the states' most economic resource. Timber is no longer floated down the river, as trucks and highways have provided a much simpler solution.

Throughout the rest of the valley, specialized farming has continued up to today. Poultry has assumed a new importance, along with dairy farming, fruits, and vegetables. Tobacco, although still considered a significant agricultural export of the valley, has declined in importance.

While tobacco fields are still to be seen from Portland, Connecticut, up to Deerfield, Massachusetts, the actual acreage under cultivation in 1982 was only 3,480 acres, as compared to 17,100 acres in 1952, and the future does not appear to be promising.

The affluence of the postwar years has not been without its problems. In the metropolitan areas of Hartford, Springfield, and Holyoke, as elsewhere, much of the prosperous middle class sought out a more comfortable living in the suburbs away from the river. Their places were taken by poor minority groups from faraway places like the deep south and overpopulated Puerto Rico, who were seeking ephemeral opportunities to improve their hard lot. Between 1960 and 1970, Connecticut's black population increased from 111,000 to 196,000 and almost 100,000 Puerto Ricans arrived in Connecticut during the same period. Unfortunately, they found few opportunities, wretched housing conditions, and racial bitterness, which led, in some cases, to confrontations and rioting.

Generally, however, the post-World War II days in the river valley have been a time of prosperity. Higher pay, much improved working conditions, and considerably more free time brought in a new emphasis on "the quality of life." Vacations became more extended, and travel became commonplace. Leisure activities expanded greatly, and the outdoor life, with its boating, sailing, camping, hiking, and fishing, formerly enjoyed only by a privileged few, now came within the reach of most. There was a new awareness of the environment and with it came the desire to make the river what it once was.

Since the 1800s, Connecticut Valley tobacco cultivation has been concentrated on the broad leaf used for the wrapping of cigars. Since 1900, most of this tobacco has been grown in shade under white cloth netting designed to duplicate the temperature and humidity found in the tropics where the plants originated. The use of the netting involves a tremendous amount of labor, and the high costs of production and the decline in cigar smoking have resulted in a substantial curtailment of production.

11

THE RECAPTURE OF THE RIVER

There is nothing that gives the feel of Connecticut like coming home
to it . . . coming home to the American self in the sort of place in which
it was formed. Going back to Connecticut is a return to an origin. And,
as it happens, it is an origin which many men all over the world, both
those who have been part of us and those who have not, share in common: an origin of hardihood, good faith, and good will.

Wallace Stevens
Hartford, Connecticut

Wallace Stevens lead a double life as a businessman and a poet. By day, he
was an insurance company executive, heading the Bond Claim Department of the Hartford Accident and Indemnity Company. By avocation, he
was a poet whose works are now considered to be among the most important of the twentieth century. His daily walks of one and one-half miles
through Hartford from his home to his office furnished the inspiration for
his poetry. One of his favorite spots was the East Hartford Canoe Club on
the banks of the river which he so enjoyed.

Once the river was perceived not only as an economic resource, but,
even more, as an amenity of life to be valued for its beauty, environmental
contributions, and recreational opportunities, various concerned groups
were spurred into action. Thanks to them, in 1972, the river was thirty
percent cleaner than it had been six years before, and by 1980 nearly
eighty percent of the river's length was safely swimmable.

As early as 1952, a group of Connecticut valley businessmen and con-
servationists, principally from the Massachusetts river communities and
Hartford, formed the Connecticut River Watershed Council to clean up
the river, restore its wildlife, and preserve the wetlands and forests. The
council sponsored legislation designed to achieve these purposes and
was successful in securing the enactment of stringent laws and regulations against pollution and for the preservation of wetlands and wildlife.

Since the Council's conception, nearly one hundred municipal sewage treatment plants have been built in the river valley. The 1965 Federal
Clean Water Act, which made federal funds available for sewage control,
speeded up the construction of these plants. Their funds were supplemented by state and private support, and today such investments have
exceeded $500 million.

In 1971, Connecticut established its Department of Environmental
Protection with powers over air, water, pollution, wetlands, fish and game
controls, and boating. Massachusetts established an executive office of
environmental affairs in 1974 which enacted the first wetlands act in the
country. Vermont has been equally sensitive to these issues. New Hamp-

shire, however, has lagged behind in establishing conservation programs, perhaps because the majority of its electorate is concentrated in the mill towns in the eastern part of the state.

Other concerns of these interested groups are the danger of oil spills and floods. As a result of the great oil spills on the French and English coasts and several oil spills in the lower river valley, an oil spill protection plan, sponsored by the Connecticut River Watershed Council, was enacted in 1979. This plan covers the lower river and the adjacent Long Island Sound shoreline.

Not all segments of opinion agree on how best to accomplish flood control. The dikes built after the great flood of 1936 did reduce flood damage for a number of years, but the 1955 floods and hurricanes caused $800 million damage in New England. Since then the federal government has invested over $300 million in flood control works along the river. In 1970, the Army Corps of Engineers proposed the construction of new major dams on the river and a large number of smaller dams on the tributaries. Other groups feel that new dams would disturb the river ecology. They have urged the raising of dikes and walls in East Hartford, Springfield, Chicopee, Holyoke, and Northampton, and using nonstructural measures such as flood warnings, relocation, development controls, and open land acquisition to minimize dangers from flooding. The Watershed Council, has sponsored a flood management plan based on the principle that the preservation and enhancement of natural valley storage areas would eliminate most of the need for further construction of dams and dikes. The Council fears that dams and dikes would destroy valuable farm land and forests, and present obstacles to the spawning of salmon and shad.

Under current discussion is the proposal to rebuild an 1899 dam in Tariffville Gorge on the Farmington River. The utility companies claim that the building of the dam and the generation of electricity through water power would save substantial quantities of imported oil and would produce energy without fossil fuel burning or the use of radioactive material. Opponents of the proposal maintain that the dam would be a detriment to the ecology of the river, destroying the gorge by turning it into flat water, flooding large amounts of land, and further reducing the number of fish in the river. A somewhat similar proposal has been made for a major dam on the river at Windsor, Vermont, and similar arguments have been advanced by proponents and opponents. And so, the debate goes on.

The abundant resources of the Connecticut River valley have attracted national attention over the years. In August of 1965, Senator Abraham Ribicoff of Connecticut introduced legislation in Congress to establish a national recreation area on the river. After a study of the area by the federal Department of the Interior, proposals were made to establish three recreational areas centered around the Coos Region in upper New Hampshire and Vermont, at Mount Holyoke in Massachusetts, and at the so-called gateway at the river mouth south of East Haddam. These proposals became the subject of numerous discussions and public hearings. Fears were expressed that the federal plans would give undue emphasis to public recreation instead of preservation efforts, and that local controls exercised by the towns would be superseded by federal regulations.

In light of this strong local opposition, the federal program was withdrawn and a proposal was made for community action on a local level.

143

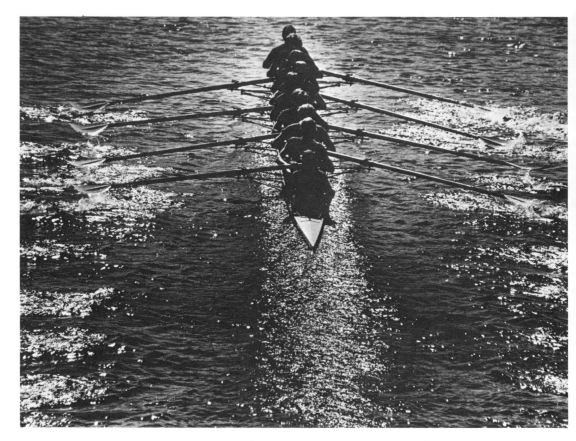

Wesleyan crew on the river at Middletown.

Accompanying the return of fish and wild life to the river has been a dramatic
increase in fishing, swimming, and boating. Middletown is the site of the
Head of the Connecticut crew races. Begun in 1974, the race is the second
largest head regatta in the United States, with over 400 entries from colleges,
schools, and sport clubs, both men and women, from single shells to the traditional eights. Head races are conducted on the basis of individual computer
timing with staggered starts, as distinguished from races where all crews start
together and compete with each other down to the finish line.

This proposal proved far more acceptable. The Connecticut River Gateway Commission was established in 1975 with representatives from the eight towns near the mouth of the river, plus representatives from the Connecticut River Estuary Regional Planning Agency and the state Department of Environmental Protection. The commission has the authority to set minimum standards covering the location, height, and layout of structures along the riverfront, and to limit the cutting of timber and excavation of earth materials.

The commission is also authorized to acquire scenic easements. Several easements have already been donated to it, notably a 281-acre easement covering a part of Hamburg Cove, and Joshua's Rock, given by Timothy Mellon of the noted Pittsburgh philanthropic family.

In 1982, a similar inter-town compact arrangement for the formation of the Connecticut River Assembly was authorized by the Connecticut Legislature. The assembly was charged with the development of a land policy for the fifteen towns between Haddam and Enfield. Consequently, the entire length of the river in Connecticut is controlled, at least to some degree, by restrictive development regulations.

Along with this recognition and appreciation of the river as a vital community asset, riverfronts are being revitalized from Springfield south. In Springfield, part of the river frontage has been restored as a pedestrian promenade along with the riverbanks. In Hartford, an organization under the name of Riverfront Recapture, Inc. has been set up with business and community support. It is working to bring the river back as an attractive and valuable asset with river walks, parks, and recreational facilities. In Middletown, a stretch along the river has been refurbished as a park from which spectators can view the increasing number of rowing events and regattas taking place on the river.

In European cities, the riverbanks have generally been preserved from intense commercial and industrial activity. The Thames in London, the Seine in Paris, and the Tiber in Rome have been beautified with well-built embankments and parks, and are crossed by bridges designed not merely as vehicular crossings, but also as architectural monuments. American cities, of course, were developed at much later dates, but until recently, with the exception of the Potomac in Washington, waterfront areas have been the least attractive or accessible parts of American cities. Fortunately, the tide is being turned in Boston, Baltimore, Chicago, San Francisco, and New York among others. Hopefully Middletown, Hartford, and Springfield will be able to fully reclaim their riverfronts, and such fine architectural structures as Springfield's Hampden County Memorial Bridge and Hartford's Morgan Bulkeley Bridge will again take their places in the river panorama.

Preservation in the river valley has also covered the richly historical surrounding environment. Practically all of the river towns today have active historical societies, and a number of them have organized historic districts. In the years after World War II, it became increasingly apparent that historical structures were being threatened by modern progress. New developments, super-highways, shopping centers, and plans for urban renewal were causing many important structures throughout the country to be ruthlessly bulldozed. Although the Connecticut River valley fared much better than other areas, it did not wholly escape these new destructive forces. Public opinion made itself heard in the legislatures of the four states along the river, and statutes were enacted authorizing the creation of historic districts to be locally administered. In these districts, buildings and houses of historic importance or architectural merit were to be protected and preserved. Old Lyme, East Haddam, and Wethersfield in Connecticut, and Brattleboro, Newbury, Windsor, and Wells River in Vermont are just a few of the historic districts along the river today.

The preservation of the maritime heritage of the valley has been another matter of concern. A group of people became worried about the deteriorated condition of the Steamboat Dock in Essex, built in 1878 and the only surviving dock on the river from steamboat days. After steamboats had stopped running in 1931, the dock building had served successively as a yacht center, marina, restaurant, and finally as a discotheque and bar when it was closed because of inadequate sanitary and septic facilities. In 1974, the group organized themselves into the Connecticut River Foundation and purchased the Steamboat Dock as a lasting symbol of the river's colorful past and the only tangible reminder of the golden days of sail and steam. In the course of a few years, the dock has been turned into a

The Essex Griswold Inn was built in 1776 and has been in continuous operation ever since. Later additions to the building were the Tap Room shown above, which was originally a one-room schoolhouse, and the Covered Bridge Room, so called because it was constructed with lumber from an abandoned New Hampshire covered bridge. The Griswold has one of the finest collections of ship prints in the country, as well as a collection of antique firearms and steamboat memorabilia.

museum with permanent exhibits of "Life at the River's Edge," centering on the major themes of river history and the important contributions of the residents of the river valley. Adjoining the Steamboat Dock is the Hayden Chandlery housing the Thomas A. Stevens Maritime Library, the major research facility of the maritime history of the Connecticut River.

More often than not, the solution of one problem brings along other problems in its wake, and the cleaning of the Connecticut River has been no exception. Plans were soon afoot to divert some seventy-two million gallons a day from the river's freshet at Northfield, Massachusetts, to replenish the Boston reservoirs at Quabbin. The Massachusetts legislators and the Army Engineers originally voiced support for the plan, but western Massachusetts and Connecticut sentiment has been overwhelmingly opposed, and the plan has been shelved, temporarily at least.

Another concern of today has been raised by the presence of two nuclear plants on the river. The Connecticut Yankee plant at Haddam, with a generating capacity of 575,000 kilowatts, began its operations in 1967, and the Vermont Yankee plant, in Vernon, with a capacity of 540,000 kilowatts, in 1972. Northeast Utilities, the operator of the Connecticut Yankee plant,

Muster Day, the second Saturday in July, brings some seventy-five corps of fifers, pipers, and drummers from up and down the East coast and beyond to Deep River, Connecticut. The Deep River Muster was established in 1873 and is probably the largest such event in the world. Here, the Second Company, Governor's Foot Guard, of New Haven is showing its colors.

claims that the Haddam plant has established itself as the world's leading nuclear generating unit, both in terms of reliability and total power produced. Vermont Yankee has generally had a poor record, and in 1973 it was fined $15,000 for violations of established safety procedures. In 1976, it made an out-of-court settlement on a suit brought by the state of Vermont for dumping 83,000 gallons of radioactive water into the river. In Haddam, on the other hand, the Connecticut State Water Resources Commission, after a five-year study, concluded that the nuclear plant had done little harm to the river's aquatic life.

The Pennsylvania Three Mile Island accident of 1979 has raised considerable concern over the future of nuclear plants. Various groups have organized to oppose further construction of nuclear plants and even to curtail the operations of those already in operation. Brattleboro, Vermont, is the headquarters of the New England Coalition on Nuclear Pollution. However, New England has comparatively few natural sources of energy,

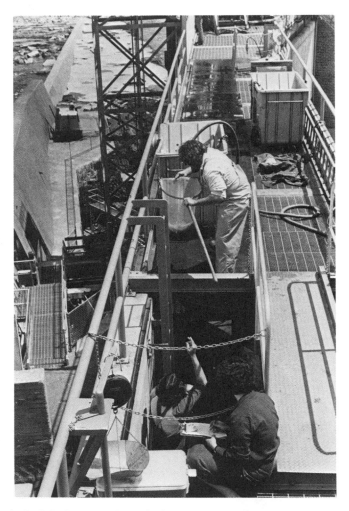

The fish elevator at the Holyoke Water Power Company Dam was built in 1955 and was the first on the river. Here, biologists from the University of Massachusetts and the Massachusetts Fish and Wildlife Department work on the elevator.

and the energy derived from these plants has been an important, if not vital, economic asset. Moreover, both plants have provided substantial tax benefits to their communities because of their high assessments. The Vernon plant pays approximately eighty-five percent of the town's taxes.

The majority of people today, however, are mainly interested in the fact that the river is once again providing them with much to do. Fishing, boating, and the enjoyment of nature have become commonplace activities for many.

In recent years, fishing has been revived. The programs for pollution abatement have significantly increased fishing opportunities. Also, salmon and shad now have access to spawning grounds through fish passageways and ladders at hydroelectric power dams.

It has been estimated that the shad run now exceeds 800,000 fish each year, that between 40,000 and 80,000 are taken annually by hook and line fishermen, and 80,000 are taken on a commercial basis. Shad spawning above the Holyoke dam was made possible in 1955 when the Holyoke Water Power Company instituted a special elevator to lift shad over the dam. The 5,000 fish which had been so lifted in 1955 increased to 65,000 in 1970 and 375,000 in 1980. Three new fish ladders have been completed at Turner's Falls by the Western Massachusetts Electric Company (at a cost of fifteen million dollars); and one at Vernon Dam by the New England Power Company; and construction of a third ladder at Bellows Falls is currently underway. Indeed, plans are already afoot for another ladder at Wilder dam, above Lebanon, New Hampshire.

Commercial fishing of shad takes place south of Hartford, particularly around Rocky Hill, Haddam, and Old Saybrook, and the season runs from April first through June fifteenth. The fishing, done at night, is generally a two-man operation — one to handle the net, which may be as long as 1200 feet, and the other the boat. The best hook and line shad fishing areas are now below the bridge at Holyoke, near the Enfield dam, the Windsor Locks area, the mouth of the Farmington River at Windsor, and in the East Haddam area.

Shad is the highlight of annual shad festivals held by service clubs in Essex, Old Saybrook, and Windsor. The shad is boned by a technique known only to a few and cooked on planks around an open fire. These festivals attract thousands of shad lovers who enjoy a fish at one time so scorned that one of its principal uses was for fertilizer.

The first attempt to restore salmon to the river was made in 1953 when the Connecticut State Board of Fisheries and Games stocked the Salmon and Farmington Rivers with 50,000 eggs each. The long-range salmon restoration program began in 1966. A major Atlantic salmon hatchery has been constructed on the White River at Bethel, Vermont. The results have been slow in coming, but at last a species which had been wholly extinct on the river has been re-established. In 1975, one salmon was spotted in the river; two years later, seven swam through the fishways; in 1980, 175 were counted; and in 1981, 529 were counted. In 1982, due in large part to a bacterial infection in a fish hatchery, the number fell to seventy salmon. It is hoped that with the stocking of the river — 600,000 young salmon since 1970 — and the completion of the fish ladders at Vernon and Bellows Falls and along the Farmington and Salmon tributaries, there will be sufficient salmon in the river to provide substantial economic and recreational benefits to the river valley. Steps are also being taken to create a Connecticut River Atlantic Salmon Commission, consisting of state fishing agencies and interested private groups to oversee the management and angling regulations in all four valley states. Legislation establishing the commission has already been approved in Connecticut, New Hampshire, and Vermont, and is pending in Massachusetts.

The upper part of the river is abundant with trout, bass, pickerel, and perch. These fish and many other varieties can be found along the river and its tributaries from their sources down to the sound.

Equally varied is the bird life. The Connecticut lakes region at the Canadian border is especially rich, but the entire valley is full of birds, especially during the migration season. This has been made possible in the more built-up areas of the river by wildlife sanctuaries scattered from Northampton to the river mouth at Old Saybrook. The elimination of pesticides and other chlorinated hydrocarbons from the river has brought about a resurgence in the population of ospreys, bald eagles, and other raptors throughout the river valley. The marshlands in the estuary are again serving as nurseries for wildlife and are protected by stringent governmental controls.

Country fairs are a popular feature of life along the river. They are generally held from late July to early October at some twenty different sites extending from the Chester Fair in Connecticut to the Coos and Essex Agricultural County Fair in Lancaster, New Hampshire. The largest fair in the valley and the eighth largest in the United States is held at the Eastern States Exposition Grounds in West Springfield, Massachusetts. Horse drawing, as shown in this photograph from the Four Town Fair at Somers, Connecticut, is a popular feature of many country fairs. A top team can pull a load of upwards of 10,000 pounds. Other traditional features of the old-fashioned country fair include exhibitions of livestock, farm products, culinary favorites and crafts of every description, ferris wheels, whips and shooting galleries, and folk music, along with appearances by politicians and office seekers of every party courting the favor of the electorate.

The Connecticut and its tributaries, with their scenic beauty, extraordinary fall foliage, and abundant wildlife, are an almost unsurpassed haven for canoeists. Almost every water condition can be found from peaceful meandering on "flatwater" to "whitewater" at waterfalls and rapids. Among the many tributaries of the river, the Farmington and the Westfield are considered the best for canoeing. The river can be reached from over fifty access points at scattered camping and picnicking sites, both public and private, along its banks and islands.

Spring, summer, and fall bring an abundance of powerboats. From Springfield to Old Saybrook, there is a well-marked channel over fifteen feet in depth, with a minimum width of 150 feet, serving commercial and pleasure craft. Along the riverbanks are many yacht clubs and marinas, most of which are situated below Chester. Essex and Old Saybrook contain shipyards where repair facilities are available.

From East Haddam south, the river affords fine opportunities for sailing, but it is considered best between Deep River and the river mouth at Old Saybrook. Sailboats include day sailors who participate in the many races offered, including frostbite races in the early spring, cruising yachts, and luxury cruisers summering at the river mouth.

Even the steamboat has returned. The scenic beauty of the lower river has been the impetus for a limited revival of the river steamboat as an attraction for the summer vacation trade. By 1962, river cruises were available from Essex. In 1971, the New England Steamboat Line was organized out of Haddam to provide cruises on the river and across Long

All summer long, sailboats, yachts, cruisers, and pleasure craft of every description are moored in Essex's beautiful harbor which lies just west of the main channel of the river.

151

The new, or rather, revived Connecticut Valley Railroad runs from Essex to Chester and connects with riverboats at Deep River. It winds its way across fields and marshlands to the riverbank, warning highway travelers of its impending passage with its loud steam whistle. Railroad fans of all ages enjoy the old-fashioned steam engine and the turn of the century coaches operated by volunteer railroad buffs.

Island Sound to Greenport and Sag Harbor. A few years later, American Cruise Lines branched out with the *American Eagle* and the *Independence*, offering weekly cruises from Haddam to the outlying islands on the sound, plus Block Island, Martha's Vineyard, Nantucket, and Cape Cod. On the upper reaches of the river, Northeast Utilities has established the Northfield Mountain Recreation and Environmental Center, with facilities for river cruises.

Also catering to the nostalgia of older times, railroad excursion companies have been organized on a nonprofit basis to provide steamtrain excursions through the bucolic countryside bordering the river. Steamtown, at Bellows Falls, Vermont, runs excursions to Chester, Vermont. The Connecticut Valley Railroad has taken over the valley tracks, abandoned since 1968, to run old-fashioned train excursions out of Essex, some of which connect with riverboat cruises at Deep River.

All in all, the last few years have been busy ones along the Connecticut River. The declining trends which had occurred in the first half of the century have been reversed by gigantic strides. These have been taken, not only to preserve the physical beauty of the river and the cleanliness of its waters, but also to preserve the historical sites so intimately connected with the river valley and its uniquely rich history and heritage. The future of the river and the valley can be looked forward to with optimism.

APPENDIX

HISTORIC SITES,
BUILDINGS AND MUSEUMS
in the
CONNECTICUT RIVER VALLEY

Unless otherwise indicated, all are open to the public, a few on an all-year-round basis, with most being limited to the summer months. Listings are from the mouth of the river northward.

CONNECTICUT

Old Saybrook

The Long Jetty. Built in the middle of the last century, this marks the western side of the narrow channel from the sound into the river, circumventing the large sandbar in the mile-wide estuary. The outer lighthouse dates from 1866. The inner lighthouse at Lynde Point was built in 1839, replacing an earlier one established in 1803.

Lady Fenwick's Tombstone. Lady Fenwick, wife of Saybrook's governor, Colonel George Fenwick, and a beautiful, golden-haired woman who loved flowers and nature, died in childbirth in 1646. Her tombstone was made in 1679 to mark her grave on a hill overlooking the fort. In 1870, to make way for the Valley Railroad, the tomb was moved to its present site in Cypress Cemetery.

General William Hart House. A beautifully designed Georgian house with period furnishings and an authentic Colonial garden with fruit trees, flowers, and herbs. Headquarters of the Old Saybrook Historical Society. 350 Main Street. 388–2622.

Old Lyme *(Historic District)*

First Congregational Church (1817). Designed by Samuel Belcher, burned and rebuilt in 1907-10. Considered as one of the most beautiful churches in New England, the Old Lyme church has been painted by many artists including Childe Hassam who did three paintings along with other sketches. Lyme Street. 434–8686.

William Noyes-Florence Griswold House (1817). A graceful Greek Revival house designed by Samuel Belcher, home to many artists during the first third of the twentieth century. Headquarters of the Lyme Historical Society. Frequent exhibits. Lyme Street. 434–5542.

John McGurdy House (1700). Washington and Lafayette were both entertained here on separate occasions. Now a private house not open to the public. Lyme Street. The McGurdy house is in Old Lyme's Historic District which encompasses seventy-one structures, with fifty predating 1900, eight of which were built in the eighteenth century.

Essex

Steamboat Dock (1879). This dock served as the steamboat passenger and freight terminal until 1931, when the New York boat service was discontinued. In subsequent years, the building entered into a period of decline, serving successively as a yacht center, a marina, restaurant, and, finally, in the early 1970s, as a discotheque and bar when it was closed because of inadequate sanitary and septic facilities. In 1974, the Connecticut River Foundation was organized, and the building was purchased for use as a museum. After extensive renovations, the building has now been reopened as the River Museum for the display of various maritime memorabilia, including a replica of David Bushnell's 1776 submarine, the *Turtle*, various ship models, and related artifacts. A small park has been built along the river, and the *Hayden Starkey House* (1813), originally a ship's chandlery, has been restored to house the extensive maritime collection of Thomas A. Stevens, relating to the history of the river, of the ships, and the great sea captains it produced in earlier times. Foot of Main Street. 767–8269.

Hayden Tavern (1766). Now the private Dauntless Club. Uriah Hayden, original owner of the tavern, was one of the leading shipbuilders of his day, and it was in his yard that the *Oliver Cromwell* was built in 1776. The house nearest the river on the north was the Robert Lay House, built in the seventeenth century. Main Street.

The Griswold Inn (1776). Built in 1776, it has been in continuous operation ever since. The Tap Room with its fine old bar was originally a one-room schoolhouse. The Bridge Room was constructed with lumber from an abandoned New Hampshire covered bridge. The Griswold has collections of ship prints, antique firearms, and steamboat memorabilia of every description. Around the inn are a number of fine old houses, some of which are now used as shops and offices. Main Street. 767–0991.

First Baptist Church (1845). An interesting example of Egyptian Revival architecture, it is very much akin to the well-known example at Sag Harbor across the sound, which may well have been the inspiration since the Sag Harbor Church was built only one year earlier and must have been seen by the Essex travelers across the sound. Prospect Street. 767–8623.

William Pratt House (mid-1700s). Maintained by the Essex Historical Society with period furnishings and herb garden by Essex Garden Club. 20 West Street. 767–8987.

Hills Academy (1831). Brick school building; now houses collection of Essex Historical Society. Prospect Street. 767-2195.

The Valley Railroad. Running on the century-old tracks which originally linked Hartford and Old Saybrook. Restored steam engines and passenger cars run from Essex to Chester with connections for riverboat cruises from Deep River. Middlesex Turnpike. 767–0103.

Deep River

Stone House (1840). Headquarters of the Deep River Historical Society was built from locally quarried stone. The Society has many items relating to Connecticut River history, token ivory products of the local factories, and some 300 pieces of cut glass of the Ansel Jones collection, all made in Deep River. South Main Street.

Town Hall (1892). Built at a time of great theatrical interests in the lower valley. The Hall has an auditorium on the top floor. Local efforts are being made to restore it. 174 Main Street. 526–5783.

Chester

Meeting House (Old Town Hall, 1793 with subsequent additions). In continuous use since it was built as a church, then for a town hall, a theater, and a community center. The building presides over the town green which has remained unencumbered all of its years by any commercial installations. South of the green are two interesting cemeteries with a number of early colonial headstones. Liberty Street. 526–9553.

Jonathan Warner House (1798). Built by the man who established the Chester Ferry (still in operation), this is a handsome example of Georgian architecture. Now a private residence not open to the public. Middlesex Turnpike and Kings Highway.

The United Church consists of two buildings joined in 1949, the Congregational Church (1847) and the Baptist Church (mid-nineteenth century) which was built next to it on what was known as "Church Hill." West Main Street. 526-2697.

Chart House-Champion Brush Mill (mid-1800s). Old factory converted into a popular restaurant. West Main Street. 526-9898.

Hadlyme

Gillette Castle (1914-1919). Built by actor William Gillette, it stands 200 feet on a high cliff on the Hadlyme side of the river on the southernmost series called the Seven Sisters. Gillette not only designed his castle with its granite walls four to five feet thick and its twenty-four odd-shaped rooms, but also each door with its intricate locks, the light fixtures, and most of the furniture. In 1943, it was acquired by the state of Connecticut, and it is now one of the most popular state parks with 140 acres, beautiful hiking trails, and picnic facilities. Route 82. 526–2336.

East Haddam *(Historic District)*

Goodspeed Opera House (1876). Built as a theater-store-office and restored in 1963 by the Goodspeed Foundation (now numbering over 8,000 members). It now offers an almost year-round season of American musicals, a number of which have appeared on Broadway. Goodspeed Plaza. 873–8668.

Gelston House (c. 1853). Built as a hotel on the site of earlier inns (the earliest in 1737), now a popular restaurant. Goodspeed Plaza. 873–9300.

The Congregational Church (1794). Designed by Lavius Fillmore, it is a gem of Connecticut ecclesiastical architecture, with its great blue dome spreading overhead spangled by stars, the high pulpit restored in 1971, and the large wrought-iron hinges and locks. Town Street (Little Haddam). 873–8362.

Nathan Hale Schoolhouse (c. 1768). Where Hale was the teacher from 1773 to 1774. Route 149 in back of Saint Stephen's Episcopal Church. The bell in the belfry of the church is believed to be the oldest bell in North America. It has been dated back to the year 814 A.D. when it was cast in a Spanish monastery. Eventually, it found its way to East Haddam in the rubble from the destroyed monastery used as ballast by a Yankee sea captain from whom it was bought by a ship chandler for use in Saint Stephen's.

East Haddam Historical Society Museum. Main Street. 873–1672.

The Terraces (1794). Built by General Epaphroditus Champion, a prominent merchant who had served with Washington in the Revolution. The gardens sloped down to the riverbank to the counting house and wharf where his ships unloaded their cargoes from the West Indies. The Georgian-style house was designed by William Spratt, who also was responsible for some of the fine architecture of Farmington and Litchfield. The house, at the Upper Landing on Route 149, is privately owned and not open to the public.

Amasa Day House (1816). In the Moodus section of East Haddam. Restored by the Antiquarian and Landmarks Society of Connecticut with a collection of antiques, including furniture, ceramics, and metalware, most of which were Day family heirlooms, spanning the first forty years of the nineteenth century. Plains Road. 873–8144.

Johnsonville. Also in Moodus, this is a recreated mid-nineteenth century village privately owned and open to the public only on rare occasions. Included in the village is a mill office, a general store, a period home, a schoolhouse, a chapel, and a livery stable with an antique carriage collection. On the mill pond is a dam, sawmill, and covered bridge, along with a small steam wheeler reminiscent of old steamboat days. Johnsonville Road.

Haddam

Thankful Arnold House (1794–1810). Restored by the Haddam Historical Society with colonial furnishings of the period, and garden. Hayden Hill Road. 345–2400.

Middle Haddam *(Historic District)*

Public Library, early nineteenth century. Knowles Road. 267–9093.

Middletown

Wesleyan University (established in 1830). High Street. 347–9411.

Samuel Russell House (1828–30). Designed by Ithiel Town in the Greek Revival style, owned by Wesleyan University. 350 High Street.

Richard Alsop IV House (1836–1838). Possibly designed by Ithiel Town. Decorated frescoes and period furnishings. Wesleyan University's Davison Art Center is housed in a wing. 301 High Street.

College Row (1824–1872).

Orange Judd Hall of Natural Sciences (1868–1872).

Theater/Rich Hall (1866–1868). Built as Gothic Revival library.

Memorial Chapel (1866–1871). Gothic Revival.

South College (1824–1825). Federal style, oldest building on campus. Originally housed Wesleyan's predecessor, Captain Partridge's Academy.

North College (1824–1825). Federal-style building, destroyed and rebuilt in 1916.

First President's House (1837–1838). Greek Revival style.

Coite-Hubbard House (c. 1856). Italianate villa-style. 269 High Street.

General Joseph Mansfield House (1810). Federal style. Headquarters of the Middlesex County Historical Society, with a collection of Middletown furnishings and memorabilia. 151 Main Street. 346–0746.

Captain Benjamin Williams-DeKoven House (c. 1791). Georgian-style brick house now used as a community center. 27 Washington Street. 347–0340.

Cromwell

Congregational Church (1846). Greek Revival architecture. Main Street. 635–4806.

Stevens-Frisbie House (1853). Headquarters of the Cromwell Historical Society. Italian villa-style. 395 Main Street. 635–0501.

Rocky Hill

Academy Hall Museum. Headquarters of the Rocky Hill Historical Society. 785 Old Main Street. 563–8710.

Dinosaur State Park. Seventy acres with dinosaur tracks, reconstructed dinosaurs, nature trails. 529–8423.

Wethersfield *(Historic District)*

Buttolph-Williams House (1692). Oldest restored dwelling in Wethersfield. Furnished in the period and maintained by the Antiquarian and Landmarks Society of Connecticut. 249 Broad Street. 529–0460.

First Church of Christ (1761). With ancient burying ground dating from 1648. 250 Main Street. 529–1575.

Webb-Deane-Stevens Museum, 211 Main Street. 529–0612

The Museum, owned and maintained by the National Society of Colonial Dames of America in the State of Connecticut, consists of three contiguous houses with authentic Colonial gardens:

Joseph Webb House (1752). A house of considerable architectural distinction with period furnishings. It was here in 1781 that Washington and Rochambeau planned the Yorktown campaign.

Silas Deane House (1766). Home of the Continental Congress delegate and Ambassador to France who gained military support for the Colonists during the Revolution.

Isaac Stevens House (1788). With a collection of children's clothes and toys.

Old Academy Museum (1801). Headquarters of the Wethersfield Historical Society. Built as a school, it now houses collections of Wethersfield memorabilia. 150 Main Street. 529–7656.

Solomon Welles House (1774-81). The building of this house was interrupted by the Revolutionary War; the handsome interior was not completed until after the war. 220 Hartford Avenue. 529–8611.

Captain James Francis House (1793). Represents seven generations in furnishings and fashions. 120 Hartford Avenue. 563–2609.

Hurlbut-Dunham House (1804). Built with the proceeds of the circumnavigation of the globe by the ship *Neptune,* under Wethersfield Captain Hurlbut. 212 Main Street. 529–7656.

Cove Warehouse (c. 1700). This rare seventeenth century building on the banks of the cove of the once busy port of entry, later made inaccessible when floods changed the course of the river. Maintained by the Wethersfield Historical Society. Cove Park, Main Street.

South Glastonbury

Welles-Shipman-Ward House (1755). Period furnishings and Colonial garden, home of Gideon Welles, one-time editor of the Hartford *Courant* and secretary of the Navy in Lincoln's Cabinet. Maintained by the Historical Society of Glastonbury. 972 Main Street. 633–6890.

Museum on the Green. Headquarters of the Glastonbury Historical Society. 633–6890.

Hartford

Old State House (1793-1796). Designed by Charles Bulfinch and fully restored. Lafayette and Marshall Foch were made honorary citizens of Hartford in the Senate Chamber. Frequent exhibits and concerts. 800 Main Street. 522–6766.

Wadsworth Atheneum (1842). Gothic Revival building designed by Ithiel Town. Colt Memorial and Morgan Memorial additions with funds from the widow of Samuel Colt and J. Pierpont Morgan (born in Hartford in 1837). All built on the site of the home of Jeremiah Wadsworth, commissary general of the Continental Army. One of the oldest museums in the United States. Extensive collections of furniture, porcelain, oriental art, paintings, and sculpture. 600 Main Street. 278–2670.

Center Church, Congregational. Original church was established in 1636 with Thomas Hooker as pastor. Present church attributed to Daniel Wadsworth was built in 1807. Thomas Hooker and other pioneers are buried in the Old Burying Ground. Main and Gold streets, 249–5631.

South Church, Congregational. Original church was established in 1670. Present church, dedicated in 1827, had no formal architect but was designed by two local builders, Colonel William Hayden and his brother-in-law Captain Nathaniel Woodhouse. The exterior is Federal, but the interior is Baroque and considerably more ornate than customary in a Congregational Church. 277 Main Street. 249–8627.

Christ Church Cathedral (1829). Designed by Ithiel Town. One of the earliest neo-Gothic churches in the United States, based on the traditional style of English churches. 45 Church Street. 527–7231.

State Capitol (1875-1879). Victorian Gothic style, designed by Richard M. Upjohn. Capitol Avenue. 566–3662. The exterior was cleaned and restored in 1981.

Raymond E. Baldwin Museum of Connecticut History. State Library — Supreme Court Building (1910). Colt collection of firearms. Changing exhibits. 231 Capitol Avenue. 566–3056.

Butler-McCook House (1782). Home and office of Dr. Daniel Butler built around two 1740 shops and lived in by members of the Butler and McCook families until 1971. Headquarters of the Antiquarian and Landmarks Society, Inc. of Connecticut. 396 Main Street. 247–8996.

Henry Barnard House (c. 1811). Greek Revival birthplace of the great Connecticut educator. 118 Main Street. 527–0209.

Armsmear (1856). Built in the Italian villa style by Samuel Colt, now a home for widows and daughters of Episcopal clergymen. 80 Wethersfield Avenue. 246–4025.

Church of the Good Shepherd (1869). Victorian Gothic church designed by Edward Tuckerman Potter and built by the widow of Samuel Colt as a memorial for her husband and children. Colt Park. 525–4289.

Connecticut Historical Society. Rich collections of seventeenth and eighteenth century Connecticut furniture, portrait painting, engravings, painted tavern signs, together with extensive historical library. One Elizabeth Street. 236–5621.

Soldiers and Sailors Memorial Arch (1885). Designed by George Keller (1842-1935) and built of Portland stone as a memorial to Hartford men killed in the Civil War. Bushnell Park.

Trinity College (established in 1824). Originally located on the site of the State Capitol and moved to new campus in 1878. The Gothic structures were designed by English architect William Burgess and patterned on Trinity College, Oxford University.
Trinity College Chapel (1932) designed by Frohman, Ross, and Little (architects of Washington's National Cathedral). Summit Street. 527–3151.

Nook Farm Complex

Harriet Beecher Stowe House, home of the author from 1873-1896. Victorian cottage in the style of A. J. Downing and Vaux. Furnished with period pieces and Stowe memorabilia. 73 Forest Street. 525–9317.

Nook Farm Research Library (1884). Designed by Francis Kimball, assistant architect of Trinity at the time the "new" campus was built. 77 Forest Street. 522–9258.

Mark Twain Memorial (1874). Designed by Edward Tuckerman Potter and redecorated by Louis C. Tiffany in 1881. Furnishings and art of Clemens family. In the rear of the house, an addition was constructed in the form of a pilothouse as a reminder of his days as a Mississippi River pilot. Twain lived in Hartford from 1871 to 1896, and among his works written in Hartford were: *Tom Sawyer, Huckleberry Finn, Life on the Mississippi, The Prince and the Pauper,* and *A Connecticut Yankee in King Arthur's Court.* 351 Farmington Avenue. 525–9317.

East Hartford

Huguenot House with 18th century schoolhouse and blacksmith shop. The East Hartford Historical Society. Entrance to Martin Park on Burnside Avenue. 528–0666.

Edward E. King Museum covering aviation and tobacco industries of East Hartford. 840 Main Street. 528–5425

West Hartford

Noah Webster House, birthplace of Noah Webster in 1758. Changing exhibits in adjacent museum building. 227 South Main Street. 521–1939.

Children's Museum of Hartford. 950 Trout Brook Road. 236–2961.

Windsor *(Historic District)*

The Fyler House and Wilson Museum (1640, enlarged in 1765). Oldest house in Connecticut and maintained by the Windsor Historical Society. The land was given to Lieutenant Fyler for his services in the Pequot War in 1637. The modern museum adjacent to the house has a historical library and collections of Indian relics and early Americana. 96 Palisado Avenue. 688–3813.

First Church, United Church of Christ designed by Ebenezer Clark in 1794. Greek-Doric portico added in 1844. 107 Palisado Avenue. 688–7229.

Loomis Homestead, Loomis-Chaffee School (c. 1652-1688). 688–9191.

Oliver Ellsworth House (1740). Ellsworth homestead maintained by the Connecticut Daughters of the American Revolution. 778 Palisado Avenue. 688–8717.

Bloomfield

Farm Implement Museum. 434 Tunxis Avenue. 242–7691.

Warehouse Point

Trolley Car Museum, street railway equipment of 1895-1947 era. 623–7417.

East Granby

Old Newgate Prison and Copper Mine. In 1773, the Connecticut colony took over a copper mine and turned it into a prison with the name of New-Gate, after the notorious English prison of the same name. During the Revolution, prisoners of war and Tories who were considered to be dangerous were confined here. It continued to be used as a state prison until 1827. Maintained by the Connecticut Historical Commission. Newgate Road. 566–3005. Across from the prison is Viets Tavern also dating from the eighteenth century.

East Windsor

Scantic Academy Museum. East Windsor Historical Society. 115 Scantic Road. 623–3628.

Windsor Locks

Enfield Canal (1829). Built to circumvent the rapids and falls at Enfield and open up navigation from Hartford to Springfield, but by 1850 the steamboats were supplanted by the newly built railroads.

Bradley Air Museum (1959). Now the third largest air museum in the United States with collections of transport planes, fighters, and bombers. Bradley International Airport. 623–8803.

Suffield

Hatheway House (1760, 1795). Built by Abraham Burbank with north wing added in 1795. Houses the Delphina Clark collection of seventeenth and eighteenth century furniture. The north wing addition of 1795 contains fine Adamesque interior plaster work and original 1788 French wallpapers. One of those responsible for the house was Asher Benjamin, an early American architect. Maintained by the Connecticut Antiquarian and Landmarks Society. Main Street. 668–0055.

Alexander King House (1764). Period furnishings from the seventeenth to the nineteenth century. Maintained by the Suffield Historical Society. 234 South Main Street. 668–5256.

MASSACHUSETTS

Longmeadow

Storrs House. Longmeadow Historical Society. 697 Longmeadow Street. 567–3600.

Springfield

The Quadrangle

George Walter Vincent Smith Art Museum. An early public museum in America in its original 1895 setting. One of the finest collections of Japanese arts and armor outside the Orient. European and American paintings and sculpture. 222 State Street. 733–4214.

Museum of Fine Arts. American and European paintings and sculpture with Chinese bronzes and ceramics. 49 Chestnut Street. 732–6092.

Springfield Science Museum. Animal habitats and mounted specimens, birds, Indian artifacts, freshwater aquarium, planetarium. 236 State Street. 732–4317.

Connecticut Valley Historical Museum. Period rooms and American decorative arts. 194 State Street. 732–3080.

Springfield Armory Museum. Collection of every gun manufactured at the nation's first arsenal from 1795 through World War II and Vietnam. A collection of small arms is on display including the Organ of Rifles, renowned through Henry Wadsworth Longfellow's poem "The Arsenal at Springfield." Armory Square. 734–6477.

Basketball Hall of Fame. Memorial to James Naismith, inventor of basketball in 1891. Springfield College Campus, 460 Alden Street. 781–6500.

Indian Motorcycle Museum. With early models of motorcycles. 33 Hendee Street. 737–2624.

The Campanile. 300-foot-high bell tower, part of the municipal group located between City Hall and Symphony Hall. Court Square. 736–2711.

West Springfield

Storrowton Village Museum. Restored early New England village of buildings dismantled and reassembled on Eastern States Exposition Grounds. 1305 Memorial Avenue. 736–0632.

Old Day House (1754). Ramapogue Historical Society. Period furnishings. 70 Park Street. 734–8322.

Chicopee

House of Edward Bellamy. Author of "Looking Backward," the most popular of American utopian romances in Victorian days. 93 Church Street. 592–3713.

Holyoke

Wistariahurst Museum. Shows story of Holyoke from wilderness to the industrial age. Stained glass windows by Louis C. Tiffany. Skinner collection of musical instruments. Youth museum in Carriage House, with science and natural history exhibits. 238 Cabot Street. 536–6771.

The Holyoke Museum. Holyoke Public Library, 335 Maple Street.

South Hadley

Mount Holyoke College (opened 1837). 538–2000. Dwight Memorial Art Museum was one of the earliest college museums, with broad collections from ancient art to contemporary including Oriental art. 538–2245.

John Allen Skinner Museum. Early schoolhouse (1846), church, carriage barn, and stables. Western Massachusetts country arts, crafts, and furnishings. Owned and operated by Mount Holyoke College. 35 Woodbridge Street. Route 116. 538–2085.

Old Firehouse Museum. Firefighting equipment and Connecticut Valley memorabilia. North Main Street. 532–8309.

Granby

Dinosaur Museum. Tracks 200 million years old. 194 West State Street. 467–7822.

Northampton

Northampton Historical Society. Society maintains three houses: Joseph Parsons House (1658), with memorabilia of Jonathan Edwards family, Isaac Damon House (1812), and Pomeroy Shepherd House (1792), with period rooms and nineteenth century clothing and accessories. 58 Bridge Street. 584–6011.

Academy Of Music (1891). Where Sarah Bernhardt, Maude Adams, and Ellen Terry performed. 274 Main Street. 584–8435.

City Hall (1848). Interesting early Victorian building with gingerbread trim. Main Street.

Memorial Hall (1871). Good example of French Empire style. Main Street.

Forbes Library, Calvin Coolidge Memorial Room. Houses Coolidge papers, Coolidge family memorabilia, and Coolidge's electric horse. West Street. 584–8399.

Smith College (established 1875). 584–2700.
The Fine Arts Center, opened in 1972, has an extensive collection of French and American paintings, prints, drawings, and photographs, as well as decorative arts. Elm Street. 584–2236.

The William Allan Neilson Library has a fine collection of rare books including fifty-five books published in the fifteenth century. 584–2700.

Hadley

Porter-Phelps Huntington House or *Forty Acres* (1752). Built outside the stockade by Captain Moses Porter, a wealthy merchant, who was killed three years later in an Indian ambush. Carriage house and barn were added in 1782 and the gambrel roof in 1799. Period furnishings and family portraits. 130 River Road on Route 47. 584–4699.

Hadley Farm Museum (1782). Restored barn moved from Forty Acres over two miles to present location. Fine collections of tools and farm equipment. Junction of Routes 9 and 47. 584–8297.

First Congregational Church (1809). Designed in the style of Charles Bulfinch. West Street.

Amherst

Amherst College (founded in 1821). 542–2000.
North College, Johnson Chapel, and South College along with the Octagon constitute the original buildings of Amherst.

The Mead Art Gallery has an extensive print collection. 542–2335.

Pratt Museum of Natural History. 542–2165.

Museum of Zoology. 542–0111.

The Emily Dickinson House (early nineteenth century) is at 280 Main Street. 542–2321.

University of Massachusetts. Fine Arts Center. Route 116. 545-3670.

Deerfield

Historic Deerfield, Inc. Has twelve restored buildings open as house museums with fine collections of furniture, textiles, porcelain, glass, silver, pewter, and paintings, a large part of which have been assembled from the Connecticut River valley. The houses date from 1717 to 1824. For tour information, call 774–5581.

Memorial Hall (1798). Attributed to Asher Benjamin, this is a museum of local furniture and decorative arts, as well as a collection of early musical instruments. The museum contains the front door of one of the Deerfield houses which survived the great raid of 1704. Memorial Street. 773–8929.

Deerfield Academy. Well-known private school founded in 1797, with a number of early buildings. During the sixty-year tenure of its legendary headmaster, Frank Boyden, the school's enrollment rose from 14 in the early 1900s to approximately 450 when he retired in 1966. 772–0241.

Northfield

Northfield-Mt. Hermon School (1879, 1882). Schools for girls and boys, founded by famed evangelist Reverend Dwight L. Moody, and the first in New England to provide an education in payment for work. Russell Sage Memorial Chapel, a beautiful Gothic-style church, has been the setting of many international religious conferences. 498–5311.

Greenfield

Greenfield Historical Society. Church Street. 772-6992.

VERMONT

Brattleboro *(Historic District)*

Brattleboro Museum and Art Center (1916). Housed in a restored railroad station. Changing exhibits. Vernon Street. 257–0124.

Putney

Historical Museum. Main Street.

Bellows Falls

Adams Old Stone Grist Mill Museum (1831). Collection of nineteenth century farm and manufacturing equipment in an early mill. Maintained by the Bellows Falls Historical Society. Mill Street.

Rockingham

Meeting House (1787). With ancient burying ground.

Vermont Country Store Museum. With 1890 farm kitchen and nineteenth century memorabilia. 463–3855.

Springfield

Springfield Art and Historical Society. Monthly exhibits. 9 Elm Hill. 885–2415.

Weathersfield Center

Rev. Daniel Foster House. The Old Forge. 263-5689.

Windsor *(Historic District)*

Old Constitution House (1772). Early tavern house where the republic of Vermont was born, houses collection of Vermont memorabilia. 674–6628.

Old South Church (1798). Designed by Asher Benjamin. 674–5087.

American Precision Museum (1846). Early armory and machine shop, now a museum of hand and machine tools, and their products. South Main Street. 674–5781.

Windsor House (c. 1830). Restored Greek Revival hotel, now houses Vermont State Craft Center with over 250 craftworkers. Main Street. 674–6729.

Woodstock

Dana House (1807). Headquarters of Woodstock Historical Society, with collection of Dana family furniture, portraits, costumes, toys, and farm equipment. 26 Elm Street. 457–1822.

Woodstock Gallery. Specializing in the work of Vermont artists. 8 Center Street. 457–1171.

Strafford

Justin Smith Morrill Homestead (1848–1851). Gothic Revival style. Home of the United States senator who was author of Land Grant Colleges Act. South of the common.

Thetford

Thetford Historical Society. 785-2977.

Fairlee

Walker Museum. American, Persian, and Japanese art. 333-4452.

Barnet

Goodsville House (1790). Barnet Historical Society. 633-2542.

St. Johnsbury

Atheneum Art Gallery (1871). Horace Fairbanks collection of European paintings and sculpture of the sixteenth and seventeenth century, and nineteenth century American Hudson River school paintings. 748–8291.

Fairbanks Museum and Planetarium (1891). Collection of birds, mammals, reptiles, minerals, and flora in a Romanesque building designed by Richardson. Given by Franklin Fairbanks. 83 South Main Street. 748–2372.

Maple Grove Museum. Maple sugaring. Route 2 East. 748–5141.

NEW HAMPSHIRE

Chesterfield

The Coach House. Museum of Antique Carriages and Sleighs. Route 9, two miles east of Int. 91, Exit 3. 256–6284.

West Chesterfield

Museum of Old Dolls and Toys. On Route 9, four miles east of Brattleboro. 256–6284.

Charlestown

Stockade Number 4. Reconstructed fort of 1747 with stockade and out buildings. Scene of muster and battle reenactment during the summer. Route 11. 826–5516.

Claremont

Union Episcopal Church (c. 1773). Oldest Episcopal Church in New Hampshire. Old Church Road, West Claremont.

Historical Society. 26 Mulberry Street. 542–4577.

Cornish

Saint-Gaudens National Historic Site. Contains house (an early inn remodeled in 1885), studio, and gardens of sculptor Augustus Saint-Gaudens. 675–2175.

Windsor-Cornish Bridge. Longest covered bridge in the United States. (460 feet). Present bridge built in 1866 on site of earlier bridges, the earliest in 1796. Main Street. 674–6729.

Plainfield

Maxfield Parrish Museum (1898). Home and studio of early twentieth century artist and illustrator. Off Route 12 A. 675–5647.

Enfield

Church Family Dwelling House (1837). One of several granite buildings of early 1800s Shaker community. Now owned by the LaSalette Fathers. 632–5533.

Hanover

Dartmouth College (founded in 1769). Dartmouth Row, Museum and Galleries, anthropology and history collections. 646–1110.
Hopkins Center for the Creative and Performing Arts. Complex of concert hall, theater, and art galleries. 646–2422.
Baker Memorial Library with frescoes by José Clemente Orazco. 646–1110.

Montshire Museum. Science and natural history. 45 Lyme Road. 643–5672.

Orford

Seven Federal and Greek Revival houses. Known as Bulfinch Row, ranging in date from 1773-1839. Private homes not open to the public.

Haverhill

Town Green. With group of fine brick buildings including the First Congregational Church (c. 1830), Haverhill Academy (1816), the Old Court House (1846), and Alumni Hall (c. 1830), now used as a part of the Junior High School. 989–5571.

Lancaster

Wilder Halton House (late 1700s). Museum of the Lancaster Historical Society. 226 Main Street.

Northumberland

Meeting House. Museum of local history with timbers of Fort Wentworth featured in Kenneth Robert's *Northwest Passage.* 636–1450.

BIBLIOGRAPHY

Adams, Sherman W. and Henry R. Stiles, *The History of Ancient Wethersfield*. Somersworth: New Hampshire Publishing Company and Wethersfield Historical Society, 2 vols, 1904, republished 1974.

Allis, Marguerite, *Historic Connecticut*. New York: Grosset & Dunlap, 1934.

Allis, Marguerite, *The Connecticut River*. New York: G.P. Putnam's Sons, 1939.

Andersen, Jeffrey and Barbara MacAdam, *Old Lyme, The American Barbizon*. Lyme Historical Society, New Haven: The Eastern Press, 1982.

Bachman, Ben, *Upstream—A Voyage on the Connecticut River*. Boston: Houghton Mifflin Company, 1985.

Bacon, Edwin M., *The Connecticut River and the Valley of the Connecticut*. New York: G.P. Putnam's Sons, 1906.

Bain, George W. and Howard A. Meyerkoff, *The Flow of Time in the Connecticut Valley*. Springfield: The Connecticut Valley Historical Museum, 1976.

Barbar, John Warner, *Connecticut Historical Collections*. New Haven: Durrie and Peck, and J. W. Barber, 1836.

Barrow, Thomas C., *Connecticut Joins the Revolution*, American Revolution Bicentennial Commission, Chester: The Globe Pequot Press, 1976.

Bauer, Frank, *At the Crossroads:* Springfield, Massachusetts: United States Bicentennial Committee of Springfield, 1975.

Bearce, Ray, *A Guide to the Green Mountain State* (American Guide Series, Federal Writers Project). Boston: Houghton Mifflin Company, 1966.

Bearce, Ray, *A Guide to Massachusetts* (American Guide Series, Federal Writers Project. Boston: Houghton Mifflin Company, 1971.

Beers, J. B. *History of Middlesex County, Connecticut*. New York: J. B. Beers and Company, 1884.

Bixby, William, *Connecticut. A New Guide*. New York: Charles Scribner's Sons, 1974.

Blaisdell, Katharine, *Over the River and Through the Years*. North Haverhill, New Hampshire, 1979.

Chester Historical Society, *The Houses and History of Chester*. Chester, Connecticut, Second Edition 1984.

Clark, George L., *A History of Connecticut*. New York and London: G. P. Putnam's Sons, 1914.

Connecticut Department of Environmental Protection, *Connecticut Marine Heritage Landscape*, 1977.

Connecticut Historical Society, *Catalogue of Exhibition, The Main Stream of Connecticut*, 1981.

Connecticut River Basin and The River's Reach, Washington, D. C., Office of Energy System, Federal Power Commission, 1976.

Connecticut River Watershed Council, Inc., *The Connecticut River Guide*, Easthampton, Massachusetts, 1971, 3 maps in pocket.

Connors, Daniel B. and Daniel J., *Saybrook and the American Revolution*. Deep River, Connecticut: Deep River Historical Society, 1976.

Connors, Daniel J., *Deep River, The Illustrated Story of a Connecticut River Town*. Stonington, Connecticut: The Pequot Press, Inc. 1966.

Crockett, Walter Hill, *History of Vermont*. New York: The Century History Company, Inc., 1921, 4 vols.

Crofut, Florence S.M., editor, *Guide to the History and the Historic Sites of Connecticut*. New Haven: Yale University Press, 1937, 2 vols.

Cunningham, Janice P. and Elizabeth A. Warner, *Portrait of a River Town: The History and Architecture of Haddam, Connecticut*. The Greater Middletown Preservation Trust, 1984.

Delaney, Edmund T., *The Connecticut Shore*. New York: Weathervane Books, 1976 Edition.

Destler, Chester M., *Connecticut, The Provision State*, American Revolution Bicentennial Commission, Chester: The Pequot Press, 1973.

Dietrick, Barbara, *The Ancient Town of Lyme*. Lyme Tercentenary, Lyme, Connecticut, 1965.

Dwight, Timothy, *Travels in New England and New York*. New Haven, 1821 and 1822, edited by Barbara Miller Solomon. The John Harvard Library, Cambridge, Massachusetts: Belknap Press, 1969.

Federal Writers Project, Connecticut (American Guide Series). Boston: Houghton Mifflin Company, 1938.

Federal Writers Project, Massachusetts (American Guide Series). Boston: Houghton Mifflin Company, 1938.

Federal Writers Project, New Hampshire (American Guide Series). Boston: Houghton Mifflin Company, 1938.

Fisher, Dorothy Canfield, *Vermont Tradition, The Biography of an Outlook on Life*. Boston: Little, Brown and Company, 1953.

George Walter Vincent Museum, *Arcadian Vales Views of the Connecticut River Valley*. Springfield, Massachusetts, 1981.

Grant, Ellsworth S., *Yankee Dreamers and Doers*. Chester, Connecticut: The Pequot Press, 1973.

Grant, Marian Hepburn, *In and About Hartford, Tours and Tales.* Hartford, Connecticut History Society, 1978.

Hard, Walter R., *The Connecticut* (Rivers of America Series). New York, Toronto: Rinehart and Company, Inc., 1947.

Harding, James E., *Lyme As It Was and Is.* American Revolution Bicentennial, Lyme, Connecticut, 1975.

Harding, James E., *Lyme Yesterdays.* Stonington, Connecticut: The Pequot Press, Inc., 1967.

Hayes, Lyman S., *The Connecticut River Valley in Southern Vermont and New Hampshire.* Rutland: The Tuttle Company, 1929.

Henning, Alyson B. and Gwynne Maccoll, *A Guide — Hartford.* Chester, Connecticut: The Globe Pequot Press, 1978.

Henning, Arthur, *Miss Florence and The Artists of Old Lyme.* Lyme Historical Society. Essex: The Pequot Press, 1971.

Hildebrandt, Barry and Susan, *Coastal Connecticut Eastern Region.* Old Saybrook: The Peregrine Press, 1979.

Hill, Ralph Nading, *Yankee Kingdom, Vermont and New Hampshire.* New York: Harper and Brothers, 1960.

Hooper, Marion, *Life Along the Connecticut River.* Brattleboro, Vermont: The Stephen Daye Press, 1939.

Jacobus, Melanethon W., *The Connecticut River Steamboat Story.* Hartford: The Connecticut Historical Society, 1956.

Johnson, Clifton, *Historic Hampshire in the Connecticut Valley.* The Northampton Historical Society, 1932.

Johnson, Judith E. and William H. Tabor, *The History and Architecture of Cromwell.* The Greater Middletown Preservation Trust, 1980.

Jorgensen, Neil, *A Guide to New England's Landscape.* Chester, Connecticut: The Pequot Press, 1977.

Kuchro, Anne Crofoot, staff director, *Hartford Architecture,* Hartford Architecture Conservancy, Inc. 3 vols. 1978.

Lee, W. Storrs, *The Yankees of Connecticut.* New York: Henry Holt and Company, 1957.

Ludlum, David, *The Country Journal New England Weather Book.* Boston: Houghton Mifflin Company, 1976.

Moser, H. F., *Historic Houses of Connecticut Open to the Public.* The Connecticut League of Historical Societies. Stonington: The Pequot Press, 1963.

McManis, Douglas R., *Colonial New England.* New York: Oxford University Press, 1975.

McNulty, Marjorie Grant, *Glastonbury — From Settlement to Suburb.* The Historical Society of Glastonbury, 1975.

Melcher, Marguerite Fellows, *The Shaker Adventure.* Cleveland: Case Western Reserve University, 1968.

Middlebrook, Louis F., *Maritime Connecticut During the American Revolution*, vols. 1 & 2. Salem: The Essex Institute, 1925.

Mitchel, Edwin Valentine, *The Horse and Buggy Age in New England.* New York: Coward McCann, Inc., 1937.

Morison, Commager, and Leuchtenberg, *The Growth of the American Republic*, 6th edition. New York: Oxford University Press, 1969.

Morse, Jedidiah, *The American Gazetteer*, 3rd edition. Boston: Thomas and Andrews; 1810.

Mussey, Barrows, *Old New England.* New York: A. S. Wyn, Inc., 1946.

Parr, Charles McKew, *The Voyages of David DeVries.* New York: Thomas Y. Crowell Company, 1969.

Pease, John C. and John M. Miles, *A Gazetteer of the States of Connecticut and Rhode Island.* Hartford: William S. Marsh, 1819.

Pierce, Neal R., *The New England States.* New York: W. W. Norton and Company, Inc., 1976.

Potter, Lucy G. and William A. Ritchie, *The History and Architecture of East Hampton.* The Greater Middletown Preservation Trust, 1980.

Roberts, George S., *Historic Towns of the Connecticut River Valley.* Schenectady, New York: Robson and Adee, 1906.

Roth, David M., *Connecticut, a History.* New York: W. W. Norton and Company, Inc., 1979.

Sheldon, George, *A History of Deerfield, Massachusetts.* New Hampshire Publishing Company and Pocumituck Valley Memorial Association, Deerfield, New Edition, 1972.

Shepard, Odell, *Connecticut Past and Present.* New York: Alfred A. Knopf, 1939.

Soderlind, Arthur E., *Connecticut.* Colonial Histories Series, Nashville and New York: Thomas Nelson, Inc., 1976.

Stekl, William F., *The Connecticut River.* Middletown, Connecticut: Wesleyan University Press, 1972.

Stevens, Thomas A., *Along the Waterfront at Deep River, Connecticut.* Deep River Historical Society, 1979.

Stevens, Thomas A., *Connecticut River Master Mariners.* Essex: The Connecticut River Foundation, 1979.

Stevens, Thomas A., *Old Lyme, A Town Inexorably Linked to the Sea.* 1959.

Stevens, Thomas A., *Stevens Collection.* Thomas A. Stevens Library, Connecticut River Foundation, Essex, Connecticut.

Stiles, Henry R., *The History of Ancient Windsor 1892.* New Hampshire Publishing Company Facsimile, 1976.

Stofko, Karl P., and Rachel I. Gibbs, *A Brief History of East Haddam, Connecticut.* East Haddam Historic District Commission.

Sylvester, Nathaniel Bartlett, et al, *History of the Connecticut Valley, Massachusetts.* Philadelphia: Louis H. Everts, 2 vols., 1879.

Van Dusen, Albert E., *Connecticut.* New York: Random House, 1961.

Verrill, A. Hyatt, *The Heart of Old New England.* New York: Dodd, Mead and Company, 1936.

Weaver, Glenn, *Hartford, An Illustrated History of Connecticut's Capital.* Woodlands, California: Connecticut Historical Society and Windsor Publications, Inc., 1982.

Whittlesey, Charles W., *Crossing and Re-Crossing the Connecticut River.* Privately printed, New Haven: The Tuttle, Morehouse and Taylor Company, 1938.

Wright, Harry Andrew, *The Story of Western Massachusetts,* 4 vols. Lewis Historical Publishing Company, 1949.

Young, William R., Editor, *The Connecticut Valley Indian.* Springfield Museum of Science, 1969.

Zook, Nicholas, *Houses of New England Open to the Public.* Barre, Massachusetts: Barre Publishers, 1968.

Various publications of the many historical societies of the river towns and magazine articles including those in *Yankee, Connecticut, Blair and Ketchum's Country Journal,* with particular reference to the following:

Bachman, Benjamin B., "A River of Endless Fascination." *Blair* and *Ketchum's Country Journal,* March 1981.

Goff, John W., "Traces of the Shipyard Worker: Shipbuilding in the Connecticut River Valley 1800–1850." *The Connecticut Historical Society Bulletin,* January 1981.

Grant, Ellsworth S., "The Main Stream of New England." *American Heritage,* April 1967.

Grant, Ellsworth S., "The Return of a Ruined River." *Northeast Magazine, The Hartford Courant*, November 28, 1982.

McCarry, Charles and David L. Arnold, "Yesterday Lingers Along the Connecticut." *National Geographic Magazine*, September 1972.

Manchester, William, "Life Along the Connecticut." *Holiday Magazine*, June 1963.

Monagan, Charles, Julie Wilson, and D. M. Wade, "Romance of the River." *Connecticut*, July 1981.

Illustrations and Quotations Credits

INDEX

JANET CUMMINGS GOOD

About the Author

Edmund Delaney lives in Chester, Connecticut. A graduate of Princeton and Harvard Law School, he is a member of the Connecticut and New York Bars. He is also a trustee of the Connecticut River Foundation at Steamboat Dock in Essex, Connecticut, and a director of the Connecticut River Watershed Council at Easthampton, Massachusetts. Formerly Chairman of the Chester Conservation Commission, he is now president of the Chester Historical Society. He is the author of *The Connecticut Shore* (1969), *New York's Greenwich Village* (1968), *Greenwich Village, a Photographic Guide (with Charles Lockwood) (1975), and New York's Turtle Bay* Old & New (1965). His wife, Barbara Snow, was formerly Managing Editor of the magazine *Antiques* and a Trustee of the Connecticut Trust for Historic Preservation.